George Hamilton Green's
Instruction Course
for Xylophone

Introduced and Edited by:
Randy Eyles and Garwood Whaley

ISBN 978-1-57463-001-5

Introduction

During the 1920's George Hamilton Green wrote a series of fifty lessons that contain the best two-mallet-technical studies ever written. The genius of these studies lies not only in the exercises themselves, but in the method that Green suggests they be practiced. In 1926 each lesson, consisting of three pages of music and instructions, sold for $1.00—a sort of "private" lesson with the world's greatest xylophonist. The amazing result was that fifty dollars and fifty lessons later, the student became an excellent mallet percussionist (provided that Green's instructions had been carefully followed). Fifty dollars was a lot of money in 1926, but even then, it was a small price to pay for such a wonderful end result.

"Are you occasionally striking wrong notes? If you are, slow down the tempo until every note can be struck correctly. This is very important." This Green quote is good advice. People have such a difficult time learning to practice slowly that Green tells us thirty-four times in the first twenty pages to slow down and play the right notes. Green doesn't use the word *relax* until Lesson Eleven yet it is obvious that he intended the wrists to be relaxed. Early in the book he suggests such things as "repeat this exercise three minutes without stopping"..."do not strike any wrong notes"..."do not pound—play softly." All of these instructions would be impossible with stiff wrists. A particularly important aspect of developing relaxed wrists is found in the repetitions that Green suggests. To help time your exercises use a kitchen timer, a stop watch, three minute "hour glass," or a cassette that you prepare yourself. On the cassette announce three minute segments and every thirty seconds read one of Green's instructions.

"Strike both notes precisely together" is another of Green's favorite reminders. The double stop should not sound like flams or grace notes. In order to accomplish this most players will need to raise their left hand higher in order to match the height of the right hand. Use a mirror or video recorder to check for equal height. Also remember, no forearm motion and "the little finger of each hand should almost touch the keyboard."

The first two pages of Lesson One are of great importance. These thirteen exercises should be played in all major and harmonic minor keys. In addition, jazz buffs should play each exercise in melodic minor (using ascending form), dorian, mixolydian, and locrian. With these six scale forms and twelve pitch levels each exercise can be played in seventy-two different ways. Of course most of the exercises in the book could be played with these variations and many others. In fact, many of the exercises are simple to memorize and can be easily transposed. Extensive transposition however, is not necessary because Green uses keys that are common in popular music. Note that the first twelve exercises of Lesson Thirty-eight combine well with the thirteen exercises in Lesson One. For students who have a hard time getting excited about a "technique" book, have them start with the ragtime exercises in Lesson Two—it's fun! For information on ragtime performance practices that relate to the ragtime exercises in this book, see the introduction to *Xylophone Rags of George Hamilton Green*, also published by Meredith Music Publications.

As you explore and enjoy this great book, keep in mind the following important concepts:
1) No wrong notes
2) Double stops struck together
3) Relax
4) Little fingers close to the keyboard
And remember, if you have trouble with any of the above, *slow down*.

Instruction Course for Xylophone by George Hamilton Green has indeed become a close friend that well deserves its permanent home on my music stand. It is my sincere hope that your own playing will steadily improve as a result of Green's outstanding contribution.

Randy Eyles

About George Hamilton Green

Born in Omaha, Nebraska on May 23, 1893, George Hamilton Green, Jr. was a piano prodigy at the age of four. His grandfather, Joseph Green I, began as violinist and violin maker in New York City—later moved to Omaha to work as conductor and baritone horn soloist with the Seventh Ward Silver Cornet Band. In 1889 George Hamilton Green Jr.'s father (George Hamilton Green, Sr.) followed his father's footsteps becoming cornet soloist, arranger, and conductor of the Seventh Ward Silver Cornet Band—playing weekly concerts to audiences of 7,000–10,000 in the 1890's. Coming from such a musical background, it is not too surprising that George Jr. was already being called the "world's greatest xylophonist" when he was only eleven years old! The next four decades of recording and composing provide documented evidence to justify the title.

In 1915, a review in *The United Musician* stated: "He has begun where every other xylophone player left off. His touch, his attack, his technique, and his powers of interpretation in the rendition of his solos being far different than other performers. To say his work is marvelous and wonderful would not fully express it."

G. H. Green, Jr. recorded his first solo record for the Edison Co. in February 1917—the beginning of an incredible recording career as a solo xylophonist. He recorded hundreds of records on virtually all record labels of the era—including the big three companies: Edison, Victor, and Columbia. Groups that he recorded with include: Patrick Conway's Band, American Republic Band, All Star Trio, Green Brothers Novelty Band (his brother Joseph Green II was also a xylophone soloist, composer and percussionist), Earl Fuller's Rector House Orchestra, Fred Van Eps Quartet, Imperial Marimba Band, Happy Six, and the Yerkes Jazzarimba Orchestra.

In 1928 Lew Green, Sr. (much younger than his brothers George, Jr. and Joseph II) joined his brothers to hit the "big time." Lew played percussion but favored the banjo and guitar. The three Green brothers were the original sound music crew for the first three Walt Disney cartoons. In 1946, G. H. Green retired from music and began a second career as a commercial artist, illustrator, and cartoonist. It is sad that George Hamilton Green, Jr. passed away in 1970—just a few years before a great revival of interest in his music, and before his 1983 indoctrination into the Percussive Arts Society's Hall of Fame.

George Hamilton Green's
Tips To The Xylophonist
(This includes Marimba and Vibraphone)

Rules for Practice

1. Place your music stand directly in front of the center of the instrument and adjust the stand so the music is about two inches above the keyboard.

2. When practicing keep the hands LOW. When playing, the little finger of each hand should almost touch the keyboard.

3. Always strike with the WRIST. Do not attempt to strike with an arm movement. When raising a hammer to strike a note, use wrist action only. The forearm should not move.

4. Always keep the hammers LOW. This is absolutely necessary in order to obtain speed. When striking a note, do not raise the hammers any higher than necessary. The lower you keep the hammers the better. Remember, it takes more time to raise the hammers six inches and bring them back, than it does to raise them only three inches.

5. Always keep a STEADY TEMPO. This is very important.

6. Always give each note and each measure the proper amount of TIME VALUE. For example, if you have one measure in $\frac{4}{4}$ time containing eighth notes, and the following measure containing a whole note, both measures should receive exactly the same count, or same amount of time. Many pupils, in their anxiety to play fast, form a habit of not giving the sustained notes the proper amount of time. This is a mistake which MUST be avoided.

7. When practicing, bear in mind that EVERY NOTE MUST BE STRUCK CORRECTLY. I realize that nearly every Xylophonist has a desire to play fast. However, it is positively a waste of time to attempt to play fast at the expense of striking wrong notes. The secret of fast, accurate playing is nothing else than a thorough knowledge of the keyboard. So first of all, gain a complete knowledge of the instrument by striking every note correctly, at a tempo slow enough to permit you to do so. Then as you become better acquainted with whatever you may be playing, you will be able to gradually increase the tempo, and STILL strike each note correctly.

8. Your success as a player lies in your ability to practice. To obtain results you MUST practice, and the more you practice, the quicker the results. PRACTICE MAKES PERFECT is an old cliche, but it is well to bear it in mind at all times. To develop good practice habits, decide on just how much time you can set aside for practice EACH DAY, and, if possible, select the same hours each day. If you practiced two hours in the morning and one in the afternoon, this would be an excellent routine to follow, providing you did it EVERY DAY. If you are engaged during the day at some other vocation than music, two hours practice each evening, and one-half hour each morning before business hours would be fine. The main idea is to devote all the time possible to steady practice, and form a habit of doing the same amount EACH DAY, and do not let ANYTHING interfere with your practice. I have always advised pupils to practice a minimum of two hours. Form a ROUTINE, and you will gain the quickest results.

9. The row of bars containing the SHARPS and FLATS on the xylophone should be RAISED above the row of bars containing the NATURALS. You will be able to play faster and more accurately, because it brings the sharps and flats closer to you, and you do not have to reach for them. When striking the bars containing the sharps and flats, always strike them on the extreme end of the bar nearest you. This will enable you to develop greater speed and accuracy. You will find that the tone is just as clear at the end of a bar as in the middle. When sustaining a note with a roll, put one hammer on the middle of the bar and the other hammer on the end of the bar. I followed this system in all of my playing, including my work on phonograph records. If striking the bars on the ends gave an inferior tone, it surely would show up on the records.

10. Do not devote all of your study to POPULAR or JAZZ at the expense of sacrificing the technical studies. Remember, in order to play good popular or jazz music, it is necessary to have a thorough knowledge of the instrument, and this can be obtained only through good legitimate exercises and studies.

11. Develop proper hammering. If some marked out hammering seems awkward to you, do not change it, as it is written for the purpose of devloping perfect technique in BOTH hands.

12. Regarding the hammers you should use in all work. I advise the length of the hammers be THIRTEEN INCHES, with a ONE INCH BALL. The handle of the hammer should be fairly stiff, in order to give more accuracy. The one inch ball on the end should not be too hard. Avoid wooden or extremely hard rubber balls, as they not only ruin the instrument by pounding it full of dents, but the tone they produce is harsh and displeasing to the ear. I advise a three-quarter hard ball of rubber for all public renditions, and a half-hard ball or softer for practice. Select hammers that have good balance. They should not be too heavy or clumsy.

Contents

[1] In addition to the exercises listed, at least one ragtime study is presented in each lesson.
* Indicates exercises for individual hand development.

LESSON ONE

This lesson is written in the **Key** of C major, in $\frac{4}{4}$ time, and the exercises contained herein are composed of eighth notes. It is very important that every note contained in these exercises must be struck correctly. Keep a steady tempo slow enough so that every note can be struck correctly. If necessary at first count four beats to each measure. As the exercises become easier to you, count two to each measure. Then in order to gain more speed, give one count to each measure.

1. Repeat this exercise three minutes without stopping. Keep a steady tempo.

2. Repeat this exercise three minutes without stopping. Steady tempo.

3. Repeat this exercise twenty times without stopping.

4. Repeat this exercise twenty times without stopping.

5. Repeat this exercise twenty times without stopping.

6. Repeat this exercise ten times without stopping.

7. Repeat this exercise ten times without stopping.

8. Repeat this exercise ten times without stopping.

9. Play this exercise ten times before going to the next. Keep a steady tempo. Do not strike any wrong notes. Keep hammers LOW.

10. Repeat this exercise fifteen times without stopping. Every note must be struck correctly, so govern speed accordingly. Keep a steady tempo.

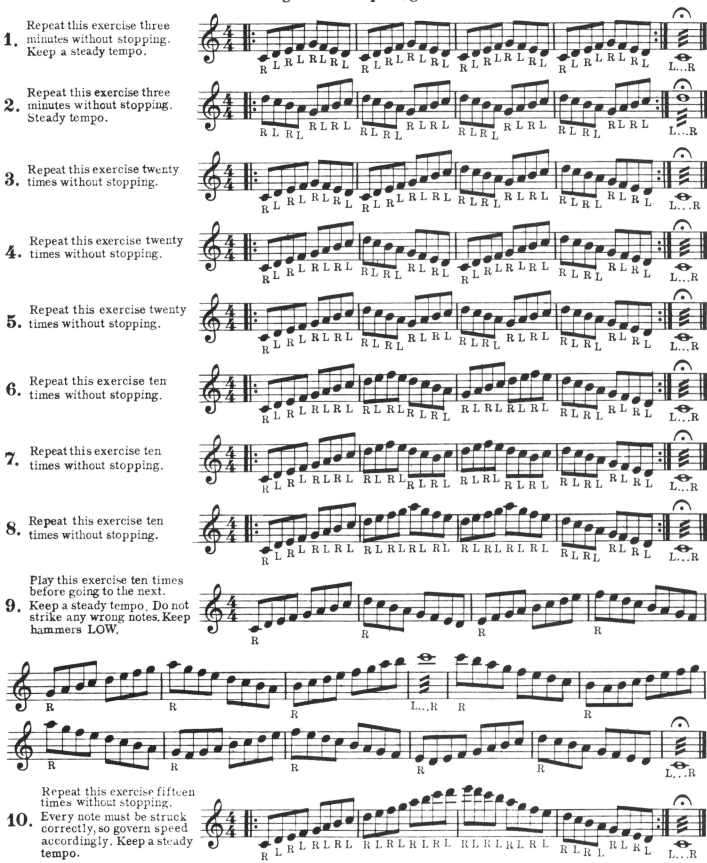

ARE YOU KEEPING YOUR HAMMERS LOW?

Ragtime - Key of C major - $\frac{4}{4}$ time. Keep a steady tempo. not too fast. note the accents carefully. If you are able to memorize these different rhythms, by all means do so. Count four to each measure if necessary until the accents and hammering are worked out. Then practice by giving two counts to each measure.

This lesson is written in the Key of G major in $\frac{2}{4}$ time. In this Key the note F is always played as F sharp, unless otherwise written. Count two to each measure until familiar with each exercise. Then increase the tempo and count one to each measure. Strike each note correctly. Keep a steady tempo. Strike every F sharp on the end of the bar.

1. Repeat this exercise three minutes without stopping. Keep hammers LOW.

2. Repeat this exercise three minutes without stopping. Be sure that you strike F sharp instead of F natural each time.

3. Repeat this exercise two minutes without stopping.

4. Play this exercise ten times. Steady tempo. Follow the hammering carefully. The first two notes in the beginning of each measure are with the RIGHT HAND.

5. Repeat this exercise two minutes without stopping. Play fast, but not too fast that you strike any wrong notes.

6. Repeat this exercise fifteen times without stopping. This exercise is very important and should be thoroughly memorized.

7. Repeat this exercise ten times without stopping. Are you keeping a steady tempo?

8. Play this exercise eight times. Count two to each measure. Note the hammering. Keep a steady tempo.

Strike all F♯ notes on the extreme end of the Bar, and not in the center. If you wish to sustain a note with a roll, strike one hammer in the center, and the other hammer on the end. But for all single notes strike the end of the Bar. This will enable you to attain greater speed and more accuracy.

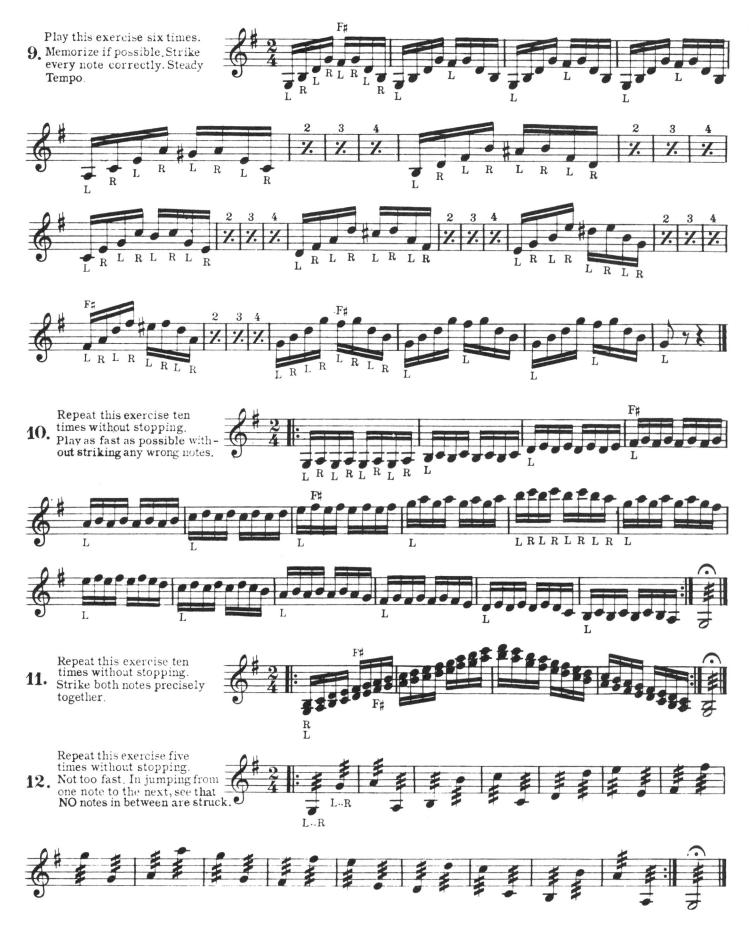

Ragtime- Key of G major- ¢ time. play the same as $\frac{4}{4}$ time. Keep a steady tempo. not too fast.
If necessary, count four to each measure until you become familiar with the different rhythms, accents, etc., then increase the tempo until similar to a Fox-trot tempo as played for dancing, and then count two to each measure. Be sure to observe the F sharp throughout, unless otherwise written.

1.R. Repeat this exercise two minutes without stopping. Note the accents and hammering carefully.

2.R. Repeat this exercise two minutes without stopping. Strike every note correctly. Observe the F sharp whenever it appears.

3.R Repeat this exercise two minutes without stopping. These three exercises should be thoroughly memorized.

4.R. Play this exercise ten times. Count two beats to each measure and keep a steady tempo.

5.R. Repeat this exercise ten times without stopping. Note the accents.

6.R. Play this exercise ten times. See that each measure receives the same count.

LESSON THREE.

This lesson is written in the Key of F major in $\frac{3}{4}$ time *(waltz time.)* The exercises are composed of eighth notes. Strike every note correctly. Play slow enough to be able to do so, even if necessary to count three beats to each measure. When familiar with the exercises, increase the tempo and count one to each measure. Remember that in the Key of F the note B must always be played as B Flat, unless otherwise written.

1. Play this exercise three minutes without stopping. Keep hammers LOW. Observe the B FLAT.

2. Play this exercise two minutes without stopping. Keep a steady tempo. Strike each note correctly.

3. Repeat this exercise two minutes without stopping.

4. Repeat this exercise two minutes without stopping.

5. Repeat this exercise two minutes without stopping. Keep the tempo slow enough so that each note is played correctly.

6. Repeat this exercise two minutes without stopping. Strike these double notes precisely together. Observe the B Flat throughout.

7. Play this exercise ten times. Strike the double notes together. Keep a steady tempo.

8. Repeat this exercise ten times without stopping. Strike all Sharps and Flats on the ends of the Bars.

9. Repeat this exercise two minutes without stopping. Keep the hammers LOW.

10. Repeat this exercise two minutes without stopping

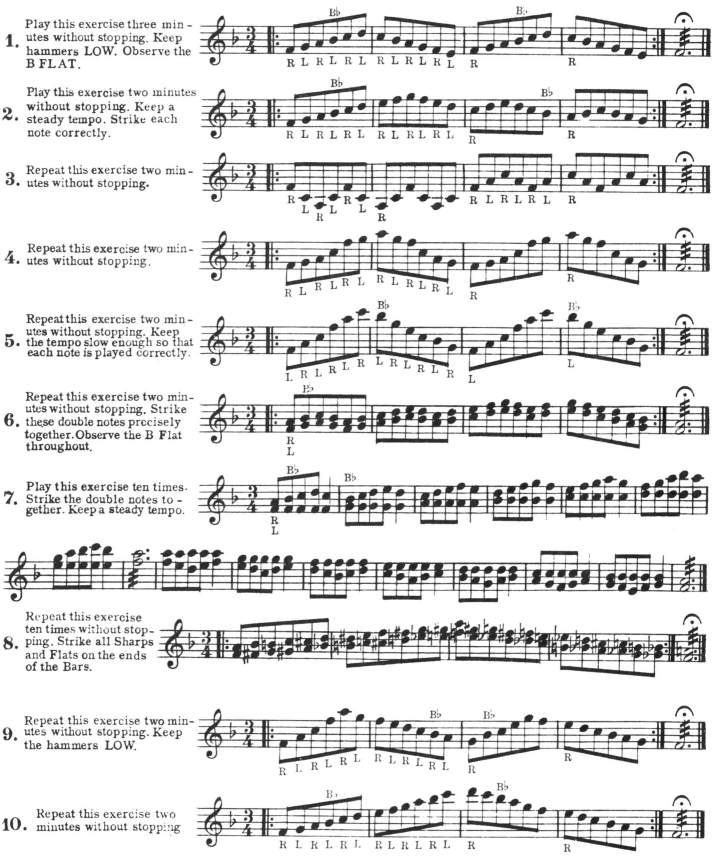

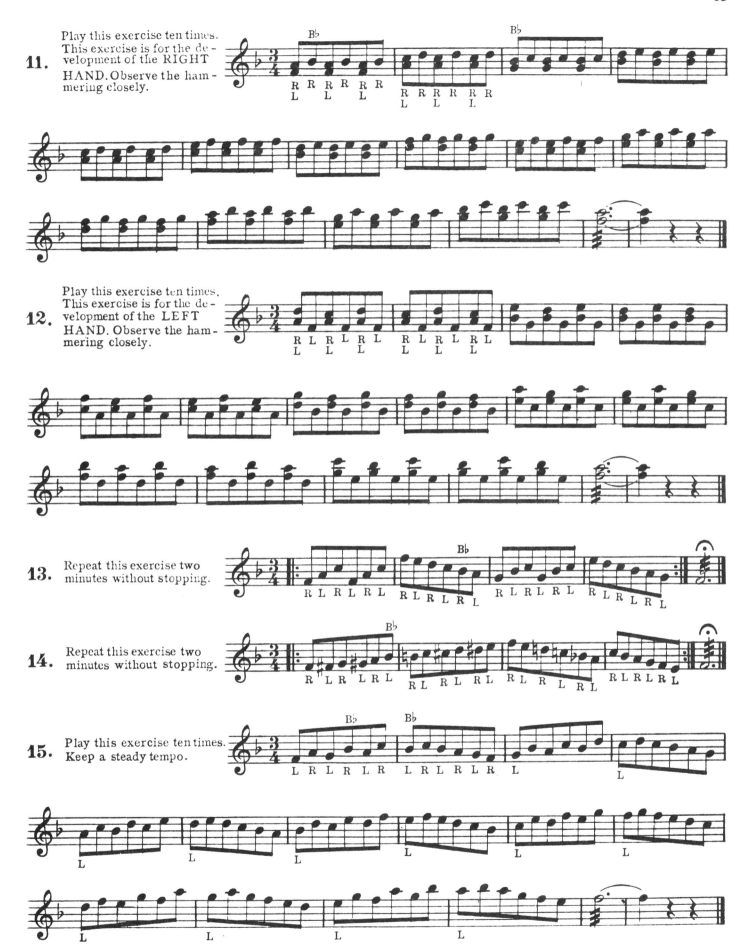

11. Play this exercise ten times. This exercise is for the development of the RIGHT HAND. Observe the hammering closely.

12. Play this exercise ten times. This exercise is for the development of the LEFT HAND. Observe the hammering closely.

13. Repeat this exercise two minutes without stopping.

14. Repeat this exercise two minutes without stopping.

15. Play this exercise ten times. Keep a steady tempo.

Are you keeping your hammers LOW? Is your tempo steady? Are you playing these exercises so fast that you are striking wrong notes? Are you striking the note B FLAT on the end of the bar instead of the center?

Ragtime - Key of F major - in $\frac{3}{4}$ time *(waltz time)* Observe the accents carefully.　If necessary count three beats to each measure until the different rhythms become familiar.　Be sure to observe the B Flat throughout unless otherwise written.

LESSON FOUR.

This lesson is written in the Key of D major in **C** or $\frac{4}{4}$ time. The exercises contain dotted eighth notes and sixteenth notes. In the Key of D major, the notes C and F must always be played C sharp and F sharp unless otherwise written.

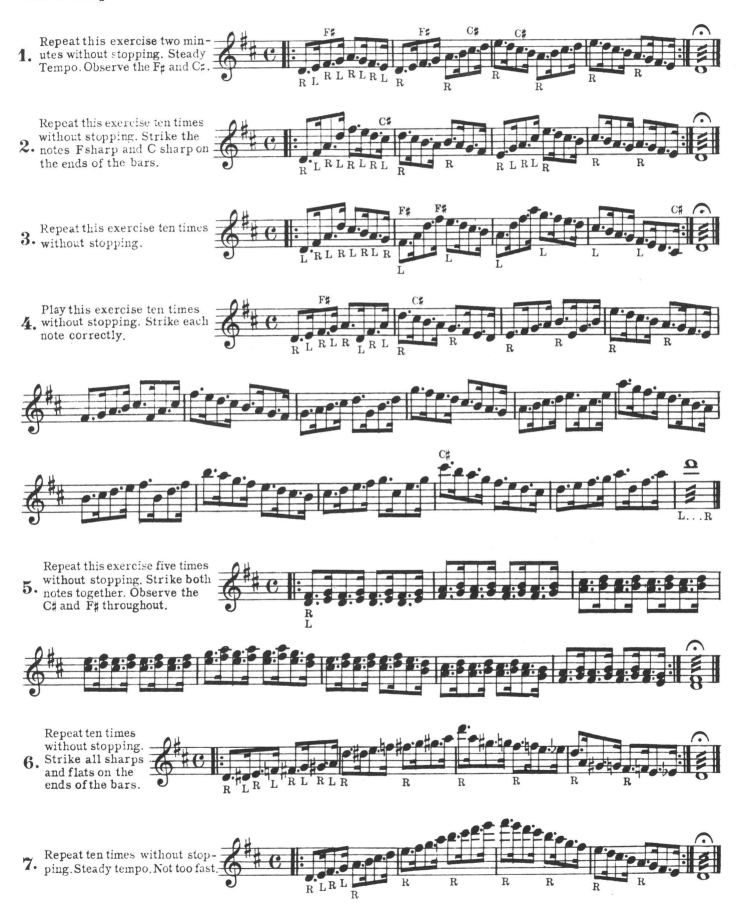

1. Repeat this exercise two minutes without stopping. Steady Tempo. Observe the F♯ and C♯.

2. Repeat this exercise ten times without stopping. Strike the notes F sharp and C sharp on the ends of the bars.

3. Repeat this exercise ten times without stopping.

4. Play this exercise ten times without stopping. Strike each note correctly.

5. Repeat this exercise five times without stopping. Strike both notes together. Observe the C♯ and F♯ throughout.

6. Repeat ten times without stopping. Strike all sharps and flats on the ends of the bars.

7. Repeat ten times without stopping. Steady tempo. Not too fast.

16 My suggestion regarding the following exercises is to play them at a very slow, **even tempo** for the first few times. Then as you become familiar with them, gradually increase the speed. Remember, that each note must be struck correctly. Nothing will be gained by striking wrong notes.

8. Play this exercise ten times. Keep a steady tempo. Not too fast.

9. Repeat this exercise ten times without stopping. Play slow at first until you become familiar with the notes.

10. Play this exercise ten times. Give the same count to the measures containing the whole notes as you do to the measures containing the dotted eighth notes.

Remember to strike the sharps and flats on the ends of the bars.
If you have trouble reading the correct notes at a fast tempo, slow down the tempo.

Ragtime- Key of D major - **C** or $\frac{4}{4}$ time. **Keep a steady tempo, and note the accents carefuly.**

1. R. Play this exercise ten times.

2. R. Repeat this exercise ten times without stopping. Strike the double notes together.

3. R. Repeat this exercise ten times without stopping. The first measure contains dotted notes, and the second measure does not. Observe this when practicing.

4. R. Repeat this exercise ten times without stopping.

Are you striking the sharp and flat notes on the ends of the bars? When practicing the following exercise, be sure that you play dotted eighth notes in the first measure and straight eighth notes in the second measure, and so on throughout the entire exercise.

5. R. Repeat this exercise six times taking the first ending five times and the last ending once. Keep a steady tempo.

In the Key of D major, always play the notes C and F as C♯ and F♯ unless otherwise written.

LESSON FIVE.

This lesson is written in the Key of B Flat major in $\frac{4}{4}$ time. The exercises are composed of six-teenth notes. When playing in the Key of B Flat major, the notes B and E must always be played as B Flat and E Flat, unless otherwise written. Practice the following exercises slowly at first until you become familiar with them.

1. Repeat this exercise two min-utes without stopping. Keep hammers LOW.

2. Repeat this exercise two min-utes without stopping. Keep a steady tempo.

3. Repeat this exercise two min-utes without stopping.

4. Repeat this exercise two min-utes without stopping. Do not strike any wrong notes.

5. Repeat this exercise two min-utes without stopping. Memo-rize and strike every note cor-rectly.

6. Repeat this exercise two min-utes without stopping.

7. Repeat this exercise two min-utes without stopping.

8. Repeat this exercise two min-utes without stopping. Keep a steady tempo.

9. Repeat this exercise two min-utes without stopping. Keep the hammers LOW and strike all Sharps and Flats on the ends of the bars.

10. Play this exercise ten times. These double notes must be struck precisely together. Steady tempo and not too fast.

The following exercise is an excellent study to develop smoothness and accuracy.   Exercises 11-A. and 11-B. are preparatory to exercise 11 and should be practiced several times each. This exercise should be memorized, and played as smooth as possible.

11.A. Play this exercise ten times.

11.B. Play this exercise ten times

11.

dim.

Ragtime - Key of B Flat major - $\frac{4}{4}$ time. Keep a steady tempo. Be sure and observe the notes B flat and E flat wherever they appear. memorize if possible. The idea of all of these ragtime exercises is to keep practicing these different rhythms until you develop a certain amount of natural rhythm. Later on in the lessons that follow, you will be taught how to apply them to different melodies. But you must first learn the different rhythms.

1.R. Repeat this exercise two minutes without stopping. Keep a steady tempo.

2.R. Repeat this exercise two minutes without stopping. Note the accents.

3.R. Repeat this exercise two minutes without stopping Strike every note correctly.

4.R. Play this exercise ten times. Give the same count to the measures containing the whole notes as you do to the measures containing the eighth notes.

5.R. Repeat this exercise two minutes without stopping. Be sure and observe the quarter-notes. Count four in each measure if necessary.

6.R. Play this exercise ten times. Memorize.

Are you occasionaly striking wrong notes? If you are, slow down the tempo until every note can be struck correctly. This is very important.

This lesson is written in the Key of E FLAT MAJOR in $\frac{4}{4}$ or **C** *(common)* TIME. When first playing over these exercises, keep a SLOW, STEADY TEMPO, until you become somewhat familiar with them. Remember that in the Key of E FLAT major, the notes B, E and A should always be played as B flat, E flat and A flat unless written otherwise.

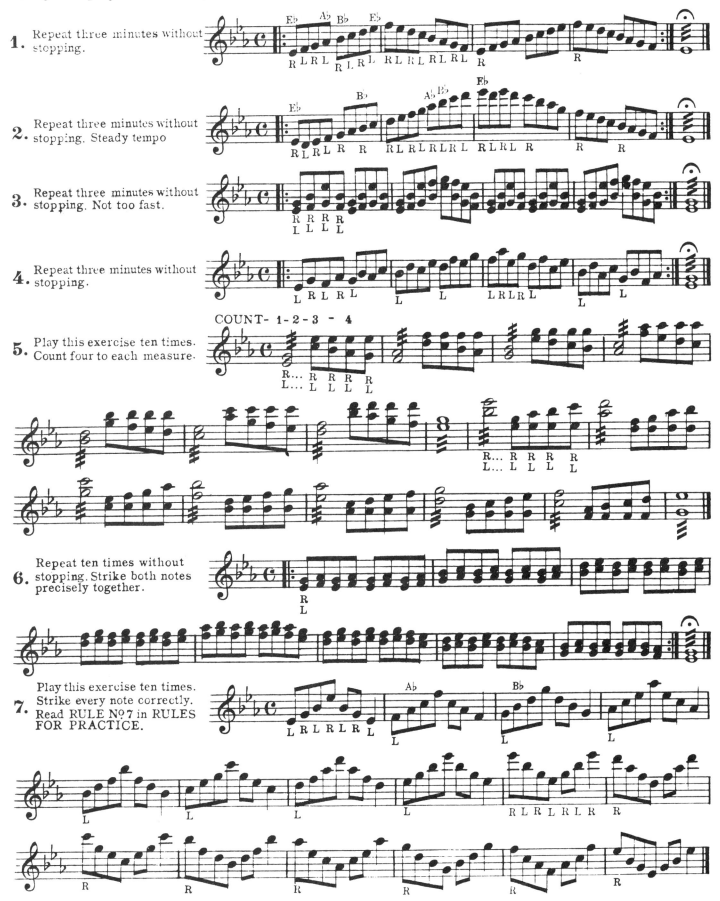

1. Repeat three minutes without stopping.

2. Repeat three minutes without stopping. Steady tempo

3. Repeat three minutes without stopping. Not too fast.

4. Repeat three minutes without stopping.

5. Play this exercise ten times. Count four to each measure.

6. Repeat ten times without stopping. Strike both notes precisely together.

7. Play this exercise ten times. Strike every note correctly. Read RULE Nº 7 in RULES FOR PRACTICE.

The following exercise is an excellent study to develop a smooth technique. Keep a *Slow Steady Tempo* at first until you become familiar with this exercise. Strike every note correctly regardless of how slow a tempo you will be required to keep. Keep the hammers LOW. Strike the sharps and flats on the ends of the bars. Memorize if possible.

BE SURE TO OBSERVE B FLAT, E FLAT AND A FLAT THROUGHOUT THIS EXERCISE.

READ RULES Nos 3, 4 and 9 in the RULES for PRACTICE.

Ragtime- Key of E Flat major. Keep a steady tempo, not too fast and note the accents care-fully. Play slow enough at first so as to be able to strike each note correctly. If necessary, count four beats to each measure.

NOTE- When practicing ragtime exercises, do not strike the accented notes too hard. The accents are mainly to bring out the rhythm, and should be struck only a trifle harder than the other notes.

LESSON SEVEN

This lesson is written in the Key of A major in $\frac{6}{8}$ time, and the exercises contained herein are composed of eighth notes. Strike every note correctly. Do not attempt to RUSH the tempo. Remember, that the notes F, C, and G should be played F sharp, C sharp and G sharp, unless written otherwise.

Remember, when practicing, always strike the sharps and flats on the ends of the bars. This will give you greater speed and more accuracy. Keep hammers LOW.

7. Play this exercise ten times.
Strike each note correctly.

The following exercises below are excellent studies for the individual development of each hand. Note the hammering carefully. Exercise 8 is all RIGHT HAND practice and Exercise 9 is all LEFT HAND practice. Keep a steady tempo, and do not attempt to play them too fast. Strike each note correctly and the same time maintain a STEADY TEMPO, no matter how slow.

8. Play this exercise ten times.
Memorize.

9. Play this exercise ten times.
Memorize.

Did you read the RULES FOR PRACTICE before starting this lesson?

Ragtime - Key of A major in $\frac{4}{4}$ or ℂ (*common*) time. The exercises written below contain TRIP-
LETS, and dotted eighth notes. A TRIPLET is a group of three notes, played in the time of two
of the same value. Count four to each measure, if necessary, until you are familiar with the time
value of the triplets.

Are you devoting all the time possible to Practice?
The more you pratice, the quicker you will gain results.

LESSON EIGHT

This lesson is written in the Key of B flat major *(two flats)* and the notes contained herein are SIXTEENTH notes. By giving THREE counts to each measure, each group of four sixteenth notes will receive ONE count. Remember when playing in the Key of B FLAT major, the notes B and E must always be played as B flat and E flat, unless written otherwise. Play these exercises SLOW at first so as to enable you to strike each note correctly. Then increase the tempo as you become more familiar with the exercises.

1. Repeat this exercise three minutes without stopping. Keep a steady tempo. Count THREE to each measure.

2. Repeat this exercise three minutes without stopping. Strike each note correctly. Play slow enough to do so.

3. Repeat this exercise three minutes without stopping. Strike these double notes precisely together.

4. Play this exercise at least ten times. Count THREE to each measure. Keep the hammers and hands LOW. Steady tempo.

5. Repeat this exercise fifteen times without stopping. To gain the proper results from this exercise, each note MUST be struck correctly, so govern speed accordingly.

28 The following exercise is one of the best studies ever written for the Xylophone. By all means memorize this exercise, so that you can look down at the Keyboard and work up a fast speed. Count THREE to each measure. Keep a steady tempo. Strike every note correctly.

Ragtime – Key of B FLAT major – ¢ time, play the same as 4/4 time. Keep a steady tempo - not too fast. Observe the B FLAT and E FLAT throughout. Strike the FLATS on the ends of the bars. Memorize these different rhythms, as later on, in the lessons which follow, you will be taught how to improvise and apply them to different melodies, so obtain a thorough knowledge of them first.

The following exercise will give an idea as to how this ragtime rhythm can be applied to melody form. This idea can be applied to any sustained melody which contains whole notes in any Key. Simply get your melody note, and which ever note below may harmonize, then instead of sustaining the two notes with a ROLL, apply this ragtime rhythm.

LESSON NINE

This lesson is written in the Key of C major in ℂ or 4/4 time and the notes contained herein are THIRTY-SECOND NOTES. This lesson is to develop SPEED and the exercises should be practiced as fast as possible without striking any wrong notes. To obtain speed, the hammers must be kept LOW, and flexible WRIST must be employed. Read rules 2-3-4-5-6 and 7 in the RULES FOR PRACTICE before starting this lesson. When practicing these exercises, give four counts to each measure.

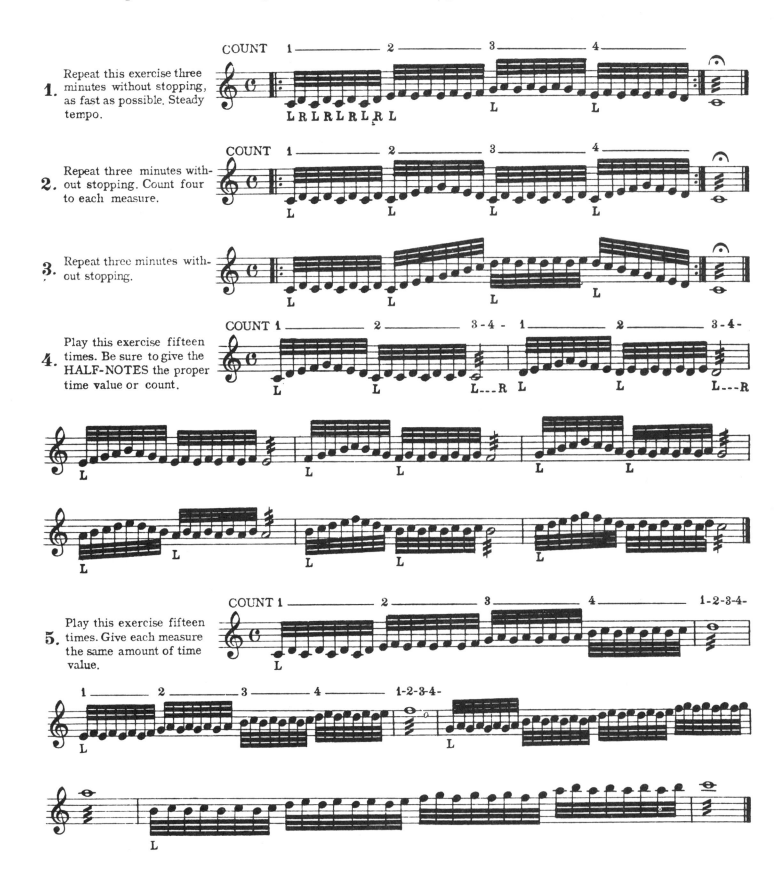

1. Repeat this exercise three minutes without stopping, as fast as possible. Steady tempo.

2. Repeat three minutes without stopping. Count four to each measure.

3. Repeat three minutes without stopping.

4. Play this exercise fifteen times. Be sure to give the HALF-NOTES the proper time value or count.

5. Play this exercise fifteen times. Give each measure the same amount of time value.

6.—This exercise is for the development of speed and accuracy. Count four to each measure. Practice as fast as possible without striking any wrong notes. When playing this exercise fast, there is a tendency to MISS the first note of each group. Watch this carefully. Memorize this exercise if possible.

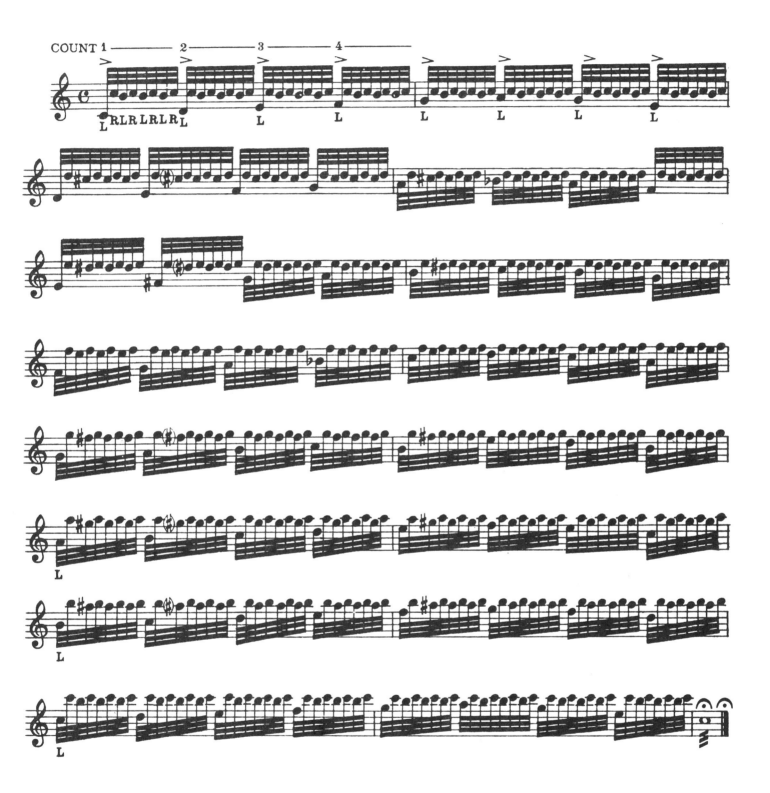

The above exercise may also be practiced in the following manner. This will give more practice to the LEFT HAND.

Ragtime. Key of C Major - C or 4/4 time. The following exercise is written in melody form, and each measure contains the same formation of notes and the same rhythm throughout. Practice slowly at first and memorize, if possible. This exercise must be played many times each day to obtain the best results. The more practice you devote to these exercises now, the better you will be able to apply these different rhythms to melodies later on.

This lesson is written in the Key of D major, and the notes contained herein are SIXTEENTH NOTES. These exercises are to develop SPEED, so first memorize them, and then practice them as fast as possible, at the same time striking every note correctly. Do not attempt to play LOUD, as loud playing retards the speed, due to the hammers being raised higher. Keep the hammers LOW and play soft, and more speed will be gained. Count four to each measure first, and then as you increase the tempo, count two.

1. Repeat this exercise three minutes without stopping. Steady tempo.

2. Repeat this exercise three minutes without stopping. Keep the hammers LOW.

3. Repeat three minutes without stopping.

The following exercise is an excellent study in broken chords, and this exercise should be practiced until it can be played perfectly smooth, and at a very fast tempo. A good way to memorize this exercise is to take one measure at a time until each measure is thoroughly memorized. Then put them together.

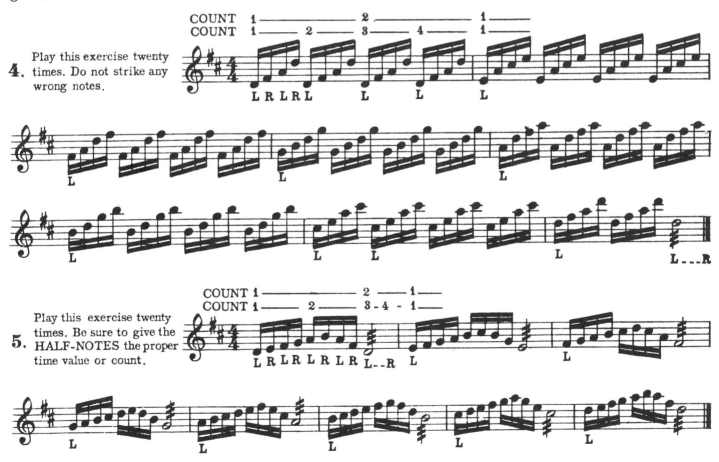

4. Play this exercise twenty times. Do not strike any wrong notes.

5. Play this exercise twenty times. Be sure to give the HALF-NOTES the proper time value or count.

34

The following exercise should be memorized, and then practiced as fast and as smoothly as possible. The mark × at the end of every two measures is to show that the last note in every two measures (*the note under the ×*) must be struck with LEFT HAND. After memorizing these exercises, it is a good plan to close the music and look at the instrument. But make sure that you are right before doing this. Play this exercise at least fifteen times before going to the next.

The following exercise is an excellent study to develop SPEED in double stops. First memorize, and then play as fast as possible. Remember, the two notes must be struck precisely together. There must be no evidence of SEE-SAWING. Keep the hammers LOW, and strike the sharps and flats on the end of the BARS.

Key of D major – 4/4 time. The following exercise is written in melody form, and is to develop the RIGHT HAND. The rhythm is the same throughout. Note the hammering carefully. Memorize.

This lesson is written in the Key of C major in C or **4/4** time. The notes contained herein are SIX-
TEENTH notes, in THIRDS. *(Double Stops.)* The object of this lesson is to develop speed in double-
stops. First memorize these exercises and then play them as fast as possible, without striking any
wrong notes. Strike each two notes *(Double Stops)* precisely together. Keep a steady tempo and the
hammers MUST be kept LOW, in order to attain speed. If the arms and wrists become tired after
continuous practice on these double-stops, it is because the stroke is too STIFF. Relax the wrists and
SLOW down the tempo, and the tired feeling will disappear.

The following exercises, 6A and 6B, should be memorized first, and then work up a fast tempo. Follow the instructions given on the preceding page. My opinion of Double-Stops is that they are the best exercises that can be practiced. If you develop a perfect technique for Double-Stops, you should be able to play anything else.

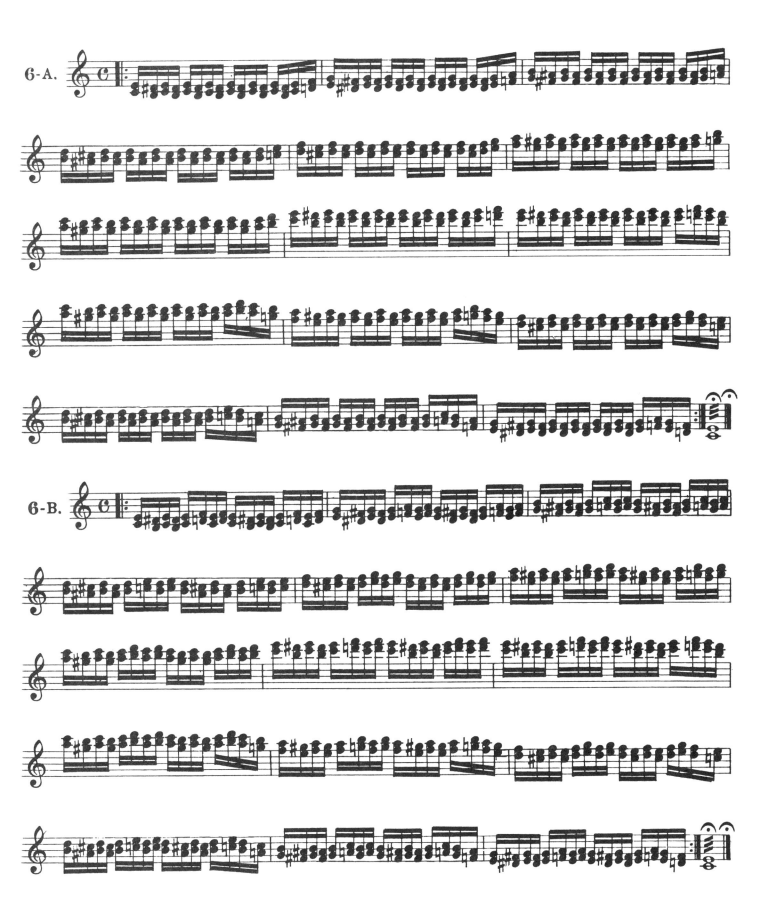

ARE YOU STRIKING THE SHARPS ON THE ENDS OF THE BARS?
ARE YOU STRIKING WRONG NOTES? IF SO, SLOW DOWN THE TEMPO.

Key of C MAJOR– **C** or 4/4 time. The following exercises, written in THIRDS, should be practiced slowly at first until memorized. Then practice them as fast as possible without striking any wrong notes. **Keep a STEADY TEMPO.** Where the accents are marked, a short, quick roll is the best. If you attempt to linger too long on these notes, the ROLL will run into the next note following, and the rag-time effect will be spoiled. Strike both notes precisely together on all double-stops. Count four to each measure, if necessary. Otherwise count two to each measure.

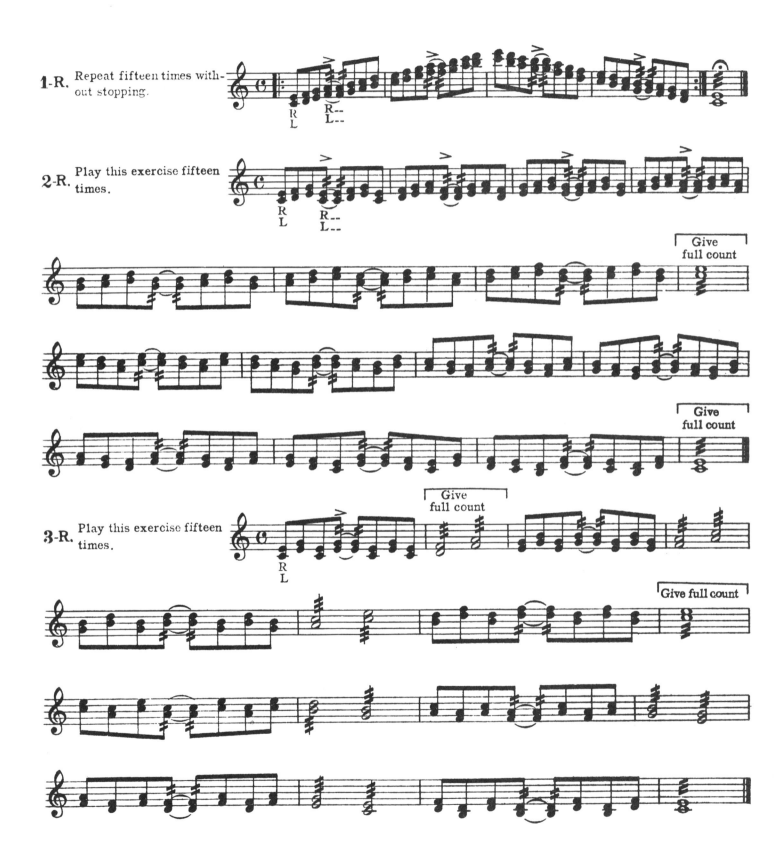

Key of D major - $^{12}/_8$ time. The notes contained herein are eighth notes. In $^{12}/_8$ time each measure should contain twelve eighth notes or the equivalent value to twelve eighth notes. The following exercises MUST be practiced smoothly, and the tempo MUST be steady. Do not attempt to play them too fast at first. Remember, speed can be acquired only after you gain a thorough knowledge of whatever you are attempting to play. Memorize each exercise, if possible. Give four counts to each measure, if necessary.

1- Repeat at least fifteen times IN STRICT TEMPO without stopping. Stike all sharps on the ends of the bars.

2- Repeat at least fifteen times whithout stopping. Keep the hammers LOW.

3- Repeat ten times whithout stopping. Strike both notes precisely together.

4- Play this exercise ten times. Count four to each measure. Steady tempo, not too fast.

5- Repeat at least fifteen times. Play slow enough so that every note can be struck correctly.

6- Repeat at least fifteen times. Do not attempt to RUSH the tempo. Keep it STEADY.

EXERCISE 7. The following exercise is an excellent study to develop technique and accuracy. This exercise can be easily memorized by memorizing one line at a time. Bear in mind to always strike the notes F sharp and C sharp on the ends of the bars. Keep the hammers LOW.

Keep a steady tempo throughout, and do not attempt to play too fast. When practicing any of these exercises, always bear in mind that EVERY NOTE should be struck correctly, therefore, always keep the tempo slow enough so as to enable you to do so. This is the surest and quickest way in which to improve your playing ability, as this will give you ACCURACY, and you must be accurate before you can hope to devolop SPEED. The following exercise should be practiced many times each day.

Ragtime - Key of D major - ₵ or common time. The following exercise is in Melody form, and the 7th and 8th measures are to be filled in by using the "BREAKS" written below and numbered from 1 to 6. This will give six different breaks to use in the 7th and 8th measures. Memorize all six of these breaks, and each time you repeat the exercise use a different break. This will allow you to repeat this exercise six times and use a different break each time.

The "BREAKS" written below and numbered 1-2-3-4-5 and 6 are to be played in the 7th and 8th measures of the above exercise. These breaks are all written so as to fit into the above melody perfectly. Use them one at a time. The first time use No.1, the second time use No.2 and so on. You must memorize these breaks so as to be able to keep a steady tempo.

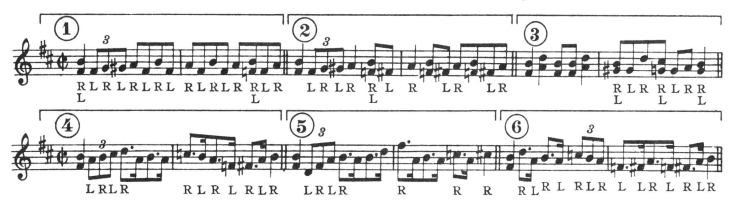

The following breaks, No. 7-8 and 9, are to be used only in the last two measures of exercise 1-R. *(The second ending.)* This will give three different ways in which to end the melody. By all means memorize these breaks as they can be used in nearly any popular dance melody.

42

LESSON THIRTEEN

This lesson is written in the Key of C major in ¾ time and the notes contained herein are SIXTEENTH NOTES. This entire lesson is based on the CHROMATIC SCALE. The following exercises afford excellent studies to develop the art of striking ALL sharps and flats on the ends of the bars. *(See Rule No.9 in RULES FOR PRACTICE.)* To gain the proper results from these exercises, you MUST keep a steady tempo, and every note MUST be struck correctly. When playing a chromatic scale, there is a tendency to RUN AWAY with the tempo. This MUST be avoided. *(See Rule No.7 in RULES FOR PRACTICE.)*

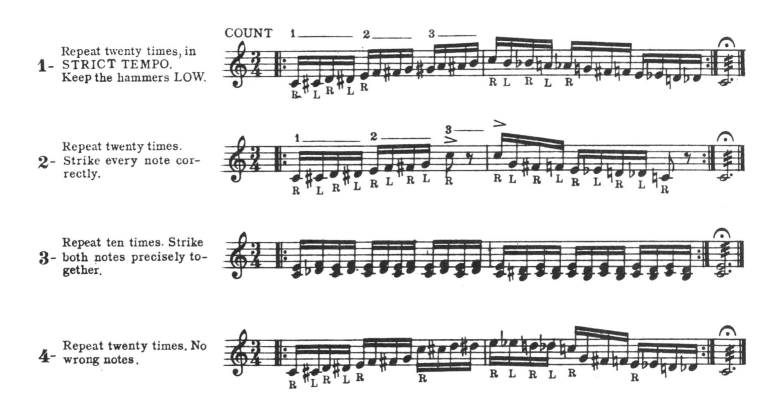

The following exercises *(No. 5 and No.6)* are excellent studies for the individual development of both hands. Number 5 is all RIGHT HAND, and Number 6 is all LEFT HAND. Count three to each measure and strike every note correctly. Repeat each exercise fifteen times.

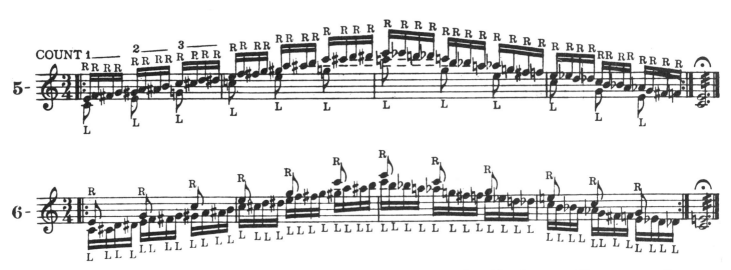

The above exercises (no. 5 and no.6) are the best type of studies that can be offered to you. The more practice you can devote to these two exercises, the quicker you will gain results.

The following exercise *(number 7.)* should be memorized so that the entire exercise can be played without looking at the music. This will enable you to develop SPEED and at the same time retain ACCURACY. Strike every note correctly. Keep the hammers LOW. Keep a STEADY TEMPO, and strike all sharps and flats on the ends of the bars.

ARE YOU KEEPING YOUR HAMMERS LOW?

Ragtime - Key of C MAJOR - ¢ time - Play the same as 4/4 time. *(Fox-Trot Tempo.)* Be sure and observe the DOTTED EIGHTH NOTES throughout in order to bring out the proper effect of these exercises. Give TWO COUNTS to each measure and keep the tempo similar to a Fox-Trot tempo as played for dancing.

1-R. Repeat twenty times without stopping.

The following exercise is written in melody form, and should be memorized and played as if you were playing it for a dance number. Repeat it at least eight times and take the first ending EVERY TIME until you decide to stop, then finish by taking the 2nd ending.

2-R.

The following exercise is written in melody form. Memorize thoroughly, and then play it at a strict dance tempo *(Fox-Trot.)* Repeat several times, always taking the 1st ending. Use the 2nd ending only when you decide to stop. Both exercises *(no. 2-R and 3-R)* are based on the CHROMATIC SCALE, and constructed in melody form.

3-R.

This lesson is written in the Key of **A FLAT MAJOR** *(Four Flats)* In **C** TIME. *(Same as* **4/4** *time)* and the notes contained herein are SIXTEENTH NOTES. When playing in the Key of A FLAT MAJOR, the notes B, E, A and D must always be played as **B FLAT, E FLAT, A FLAT** and **D FLAT**, unless written otherwise. Always strike the sharps and flats on the extreme ENDS OF THE BARS. Keep an absolute STEADY TEMPO, and when making the REPEATS, always repeat in STRICT TEMPO. The short exercises contained in these lessons should be repeated many times IN TEMPO in order to get the desired results. This is very important.

1 - Repeat twenty times without stopping Strike EVERY NOTE correctly.

2 - Repeat twenty times without stopping. Keep the hammers low.

3 - Repeat twenty times without stopping. MEMORIZE this exercise.

4 - Repeat twenty times without stopping. MEMORIZE this exercise.

(Note) Devote all the time possible to exercises No. 3 and 4. Memorize each one THOROUGHLY. Then look down at the instrument and work them up for SPEED. These two exercises can be applied to a melody in the form of a variation VERY EASILY. You will be taught how to do this in the lessons that follow. Perfect these two exercises NOW.

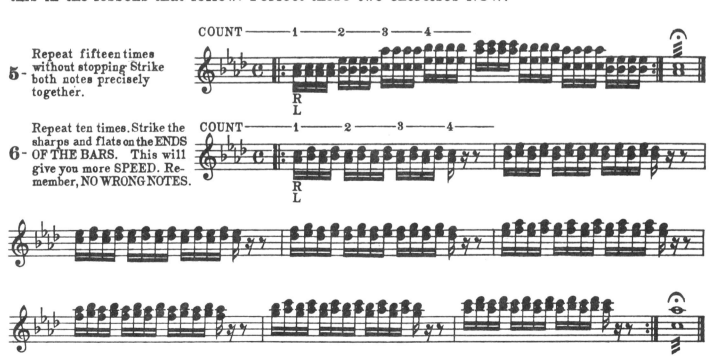

5 - Repeat fifteen times without stopping Strike both notes precisely together.

6 - Repeat ten times. Strike the sharps and flats on the ENDS OF THE BARS. This will give you more SPEED. Remember, NO WRONG NOTES.

EXERCISE No. 7– This exercise is an excellent study of the A FLAT scale. Devote all the practice you possibly can to it. Remember, the more you perfect your SCALE TECHNIQUE, the better you will be able to play VARIATIONS. A variation is nothing more or less than a group of SCALES and ARPEGGIOS constructed so as to harmonize with whatever melody is being played. By all means MEMORIZE this exercise, then look down at the instrument and work up SPEED. Remember though, every note MUST be struck CORRECTLY. So govern your speed accordingly. Keep a STEADY TEMPO.

DO YOU STRIKE ALL THE SHARPS AND FLATS ON THE ENDS OF THE BARS?
YOU MUST DO SO IF YOU WISH TO DEVELOP SPEED

RAGTIME - Key of A FLAT MAJOR *(Four Flats)* in **C** TIME *(Same as 4/4 time.)* These two exercises below, written in Melody Form, will give an idea as to how the exercises No. **3** and **4** can be used in the form of a VARIATION and MELODY. The 1st and 2nd measures of exercise **1-R** on this page are of the same construction as the 1st measure in exercise **3** on the other page. The only difference is that the notes in the 1st and 2nd measures of exercise **1-R** are DOTTED EIGHTH NOTES, whereas the notes in the 1st measure of exercise **3** *(other page)* are SIX - TEENTH NOTES. The notes in the 5th and 6th measures of exercise **1-R** are of the same construction as the 2nd measure of exercise **4**. *(other page.)*

1-R Memorize this exercise. Repeat many times Observe the DOTTED EIGHTH NOTES.

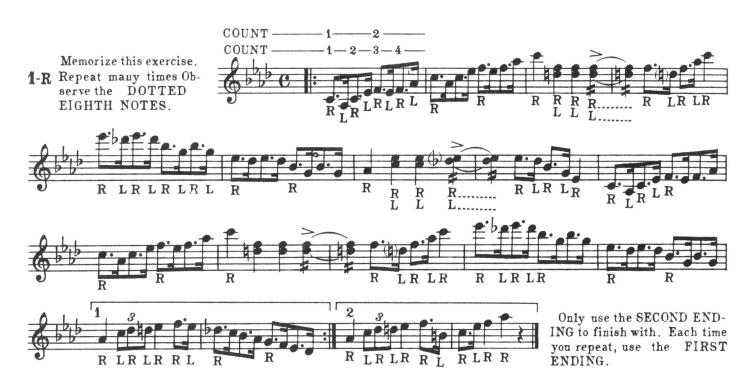

Only use the SECOND ENDING to finish with. Each time you repeat, use the FIRST ENDING.

The following exercise *(2-R)* will give an idea as to how the construction of notes contained in exercises No. **3** and **4** *(other page)* can be used in the form of VARIATION to exercise **1-R** The more practice you devote to exercises No. **3** and **4**, the better you will be able to play these two exercises *(No. 1-R and 2-R.)*

2-R Memorize then work up SPEED. This exercise MUST be played in STRICT TEMPO.

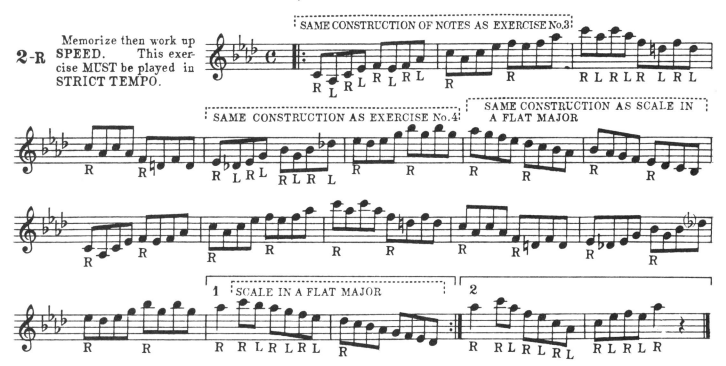

This lesson is written in the Key of C MAJOR in C TIME *(same as 4/4 time.)* This entire lesson is based on GRACE-NOTES. Remember, when playing these GRACE-NOTES, you MUST NOT take away from the TIME-VALUE of the LEGITIMATE NOTES. *(Large notes.)* The COUNT MUST FALL on the legitimate notes. A GRACE NOTE is an ornamental note or embellishment, and although it is not essential to the melody or harmony of a composition, it can be used to obtain many pleasing effects. When properly applied, GRACE NOTES will add MORE COLOR and MORE LIFE to a melody. A grace note must always be played so as not to rob the PRINCIPAL NOTE of any of it's time value, or as little as possible, if any. Your tempo MUST BE STEADY when practicing these exercises, and DON'T try to play this lesson TOO FAST. Memorize and learn these grace notes thoroughly. Always see that the COUNT or BEAT falls on the PRINCIPAL NOTE *(large note)* and NOT on the GRACE NOTE. *(small note.)*

Note where the COUNT or BEAT falls in these exercises. Be sure that you are RIGHT on this.

LESSON FIFTEEN - RAGTIME

RAGTIME - KEY of C MAJOR - C TIME *(same as 4/4 time)*. The exercise written below will give a good idea as to how GRACE NOTES can BUILD UP a melody and make it sound MORE ELABO-RATE. The melodies written below are exactly the same. The top line *(SMALL NOTES)* contains the STRAIGHT MELODY. The bottom line *(LARGE NOTES)* contains EXACTLY THE SAME MELODY with the GRACE NOTES added to give more COLOR and more "PEP" to the melody. This example will show what a REMARKABLE DIFFERENCE a few GRACE NOTES can make. Study this exercise carefully and note how the GRACE NOTES are applied to the straight melody. One of the most important factors of playing RAGTIME is the player's ability to properly apply GRACE NOTES. The most simple melody can be made to sound FULL OF PEP with the proper use of GRACE NOTES. Keep a STEADY TEMPO.

(NOTE) If your instrument is only THREE OCTAVES with the note C being the lowest note, play this exercise ONE OCTAVE HIGHER than written.

FIRST, MEMORIZE THIS STRAIGHT MELODY. Then practice the bottom line containing the grace notes. Repeat several times.

1-R.

This exercise MUST be played SLOW, so that the proper count falls on the LEGITIMATE notes and NOT on the grace notes.

(NOTE.) The 2nd ending of this exercise *(LOWER LINE)* can be used as a TRICK ENDING for almost any dance melody ending in the Key of C.

This lesson is written in the Key of D FLAT MAJOR *(Five Flats)* in **C** time *(same as* $\frac{4}{4}$ *time)* and the notes contained herein are SIXTEENTH NOTES. Remember, when playing in the Key of D FLAT MAJOR, the notes B, E, A, D and G must always be played as B FLAT, E FLAT, A FLAT, D FLAT and G FLAT unless written otherwise.

Exercise No 1 is written in quarter-notes and should be practiced SLOW until you are thoroughly familiar with the D FLAT MAJOR SCALE. Memorize this exercise. If you are thoroughly familiar with this exercise *(No. 1)* the other exercises will be easier for you. Keep a STEADY TEMPO throughout this lesson. Count FOUR beats to each measure, and strike all notes containing the FLATS on the ends of the bars. DON'T rush the tempo at the expense of striking WRONG NOTES.

1- Practice this exercise until you are thoroughly familiar with the Scale of **D FLAT MAJOR**.

2- Repeat twenty times. EVERY NOTE must be struck correctly.

3- Repeat twenty times. Keep the hammers LOW. NO WRONG NOTES.

4- Play this exercise ten times. Strike both notes precisely together. Keep a STRICT TEMPO. Observe the COUNT.

5- Repeat fifteen times. Memorize and strike both notes together. DON'T SEE-SAW.

6- Repeat ten times. Observe the hammering carefully. The sixteenth-notes are all for the RIGHT HAND.

7- Repeat fifteen times without stopping. Memorize thoroughly. STEADY TEMPO.

52

Observe the hammering carefully in the following exercises, *(no.8 and no.9)* They are excellent studies to individually develop both hands. When first playing over an exercise, play it VERY SLOW for a few times until you become somewhat familiar with it. This will enable you to strike EVERY NOTE CORRECTLY. This is very important.

Ragtime - Key of D FLAT MAJOR *(Five Flats)* in **C** time *(Same as 4/4 time)* Practice Exercise **1-R** until you are thoroughly familiar with this rhythm, This will prepare you for Exercise **2-R** which contains exactly the same rhythm, with the exception that it is applied to different notes.

Keep a steady tempo, and when practicing these Ragtime Exercises try to imagine that you are playing them with a Dance Orchestra. After you do this for a while, you will notice a certain STEADINESS to your ragtime that you did not notice before. Strike all notes containing the FLATS on the ENDS of the BARS.

The following exercise *(No. 2-R)* is written in melody form and contains the same rhythm as in Exercise No. **1-R**. The 7th and 8th measures of this exercise are left open and these two measures are to be filled in as a SOLO BREAK. The BREAKS written below, *(No. 1-2-3-and 4)* are to be played in the 7th and 8th measures of this exercise. Memorize these BREAKS, and then apply them to the 7th and 8th measures of this exercise. Each time you repeat the exercise, play a different BREAK until you have played all four breaks. Always play the FIRST ENDING when repeating. Only play the 2nd ending when you decide to stop.

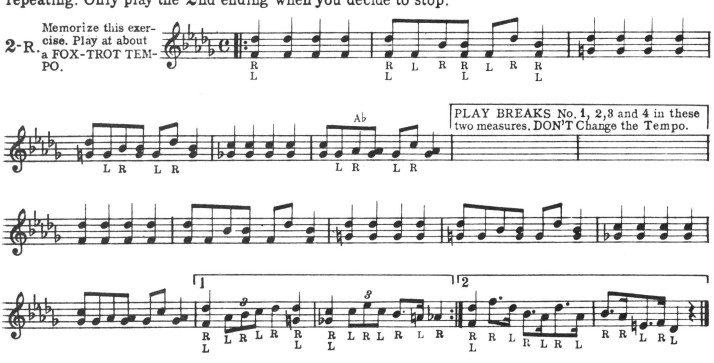

It is understood, of course, that you play only ONE of these BREAKS in the 7th and 8th measures of Exercise No. **2-R** each time you repeat it. Play BREAK No **1** the first time you play Exercise No. **2-R**, then when you repeat the exercise play BREAK No **2** the second time, and so on. In order to properly apply these BREAKS in STRICT TEMPO, you must thoroughly memorize them first.

This lesson is written in the Key of A MINOR in 4/4 time. In music, there are TWELVE MINOR KEYS as well as TWELVE MAJOR KEYS. Every MINOR scale receives the signature of the major scale LYING A MINOR THIRD ABOVE IT. Thus, the Key of A MINOR receives the signature of C MAJOR, due to the fact that C MAJOR lies a minor third above A, and so on. Exercises No. 1-A and 1-B are called the EN-HARMONIC MINOR SCALE. It will be observed that this minor scale ASCENDS and DESCENDS exactly the same, the G sharp being retained throughout. Practice this scale until you thoroughly memorize it. The minor scales should be studied until you are able to recognize them whenever you hear them.

The following exercises, No. 2-A and 2B are called the MELODIC MINOR SCALE. It will be observed that this scale retains the notes F sharp and G sharp in ASCENDING but omits them in DESCENDING. Study this scale carefully. Always play F sharp and G sharp when ASCENDING, and always play G natural and F natural when DESCENDING.

The following exercises, No. 3-4 and 5 are constructed in MINOR FORM, and should be played smoothly and without effort. Every note must be struck correctly.

The following exercise. No. 6 is the EN-HARMONIC MINOR SCALE in THIRDS. Strike both notes precisely together, and play as fast as possible without striking any wrong notes.

The following exercise (No. 7) is an excellent study to develop individual hammering with each hand. This exercise can be hammered two different ways, namely, two lefts and one right or two rights and one left. If your left hand is the weaker of the two, pratice this exercise by using two lefts and one right, and if your right-hand is the weaker of the two, practice by using two rights and one left. Follow this hammering throughout, memorize and practice until this exercise can be played smoothly and without effort, Keep a steady tempo. This exercise contains TRIPLETS in $\frac{4}{4}$ time. Count four beats to each measure.

To develop the LEFT HAND, use this hammering.

For the RIGHT HAND, use this hammering.

RAGTIME – Key of A MINOR – $\frac{4}{4}$ time – The following exercises are written in melody form and are constructed in MINOR form. The idea of these melody form of exercises is to get you accustomed to this style of ragtime playing. Memorize these exercises thoroughly. Once you become accustomed to this style of playing, the ordinary popular melody will be easy for you. These melodies will gradually become more difficult as you go along, so the better you perfect these exercises, the easier the following ones will be. Keep a steady tempo, about the same tempo as you would play a dance number (Fox-Trot.) Try to bear in mind that you are playing these melodies in public with an orchestra. A lot will be gained by this.

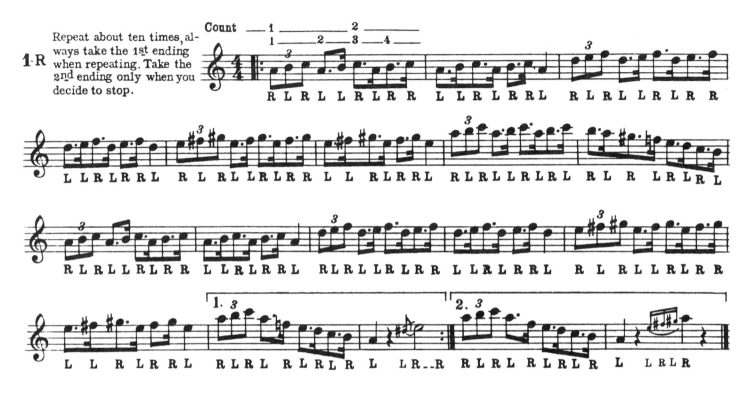

Note: If you have some one in your home who can **play piano**, have them arrange a simple accompaniment to these melodies, and then have them play the accompaniment with you. This is the best possible way that you can practice ragtime. You will be surprised what a difference it will make in your playing.

This lesson is written in the Key of B FLAT MAJOR in 4/4 time, and the notes contained here in are SIXTEENTH NOTES. The object of this lesson is to help develop SMOOTHNESS and FREEDOM OF MOTION. Practice these exercises as fast as possible with out striking any wrong notes. The tempo must not VARY. Where the exercises are marked with REPEAT SIGNS, always repeat them IN TEMPO. Keep the hammers LOW and memorize as many of these exercises as possible. Once you memorize them, you can then look down at the Keyboard and work up SPEED.

1. Repeat this exercise twenty times, IN TEMPO.
Strike all flats on the ends of the Bars.

2. Repeat this exercise twenty times, IN TEMPO.
Strike every note correctly.

The following exercises, No. 3, 4 and 5 are excellent studies to develop TECHNIQUE in both hands. As these exercises contain only two measures each, they can be easily memorized in a few moments, then look down at the Key-board. And repeat each one many times without stopping, at a fast tempo. Note the hammering in exercises No. 5 and 6.

3. Strike both notes precisely together.

4. Note the hammering
All RIGHT HAND
on the sixteenth notes

5. Note the hammering
All LEFT HAND
on the sixteenth notes

The following exercise should first be memorized and then look down at the Key-board and work up SPEED. Remember, though, when developing SPEED, do not over-do it by trying to play so fast that you strike wrong notes. You will be wasting your time if you attempt to do this. It takes time to develop speed and the quickest way to develop SPEED is to form the habit of STRIKING EVERY NOTE CORRECTLY.

ARE YOU STRIKING THE FLATS ON THE ENDS OF THE BARS?

Ragtime – Key of B FLAT MAJOR – (TWO FLATS) – ¢ TIME – (PLAY at a FOX-TROT TEMPO)
The object of this lesson is to show how a comparitwely easy melody can be built up by applying a ragtime rhythm that FITS the MELODY. Exercise 1-R contains practically the same
rhythm that is used throughout Exercise No. 2-R Memorize Exercise 1-R so that you can play
it at a fairly fast tempo, WITHOUT STUMBLING. You must first learn these rhythms before you
can apply them to a melody.

The following exercise is in Melody form, and is to show how practically the SAME MELODY
can be played in Ragtime form. First, memorize the straight melody (TOP LINE, SMALL
NOTES.) This will help you to play the LOWER LINE, (large notes.) Repeat this exercise
many times, always taking the 1st ending.

LESSON NINETEEN

This lesson is written in the Key of C MAJOR in **C** TIME *(same as* $\frac{4}{4}$ *time.)* This is an excellent lesson to develop accuracy. In the lessons that follow, you will be given different forms of arpeggios and variation forms of exercises. The more practice you devote to the technical form of exercise, such as contained in this lesson, the easier the arpeggio work will be for you. Memorize these exercises and strike every note correctly. Keep a steady tempo. Follow the Hammering closely.

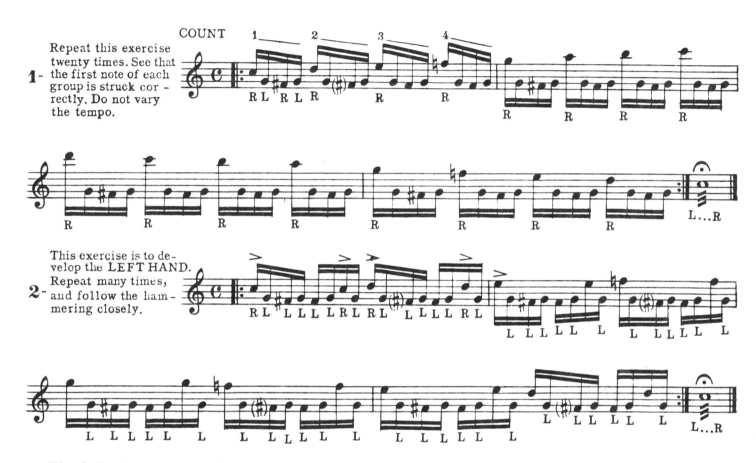

The following exercise is to develop accuracy and at the same time train both hands so that they work together. Memorize this exercise and then look down at the Keyboard and develop speed. Strike both notes precisely together.

The following exercises, *(nos. 4 and 5)* can be easily memorized by taking two measures at a time and memorize. Take the first two measures and learn them thoroughly, then take the next two measures, and so on. My reason for advising the pupil to memorize these exercises is that by looking down at the Keyboard will enable him to develop more speed and at the same time play accurately. Memorizing will not affect sight reading at all, as you are compelled to read the exercise many times before you are able to memorize it, therefore you are getting the Practice of sight-reading as you go along.

Ragtime – Key of C MAJOR – C TIME *(same as $\frac{4}{4}$ time)* Play the same tempo as a FOX-TROT played for dancing. The following exercise *(no. 1-R)* will give a good idea as to improvising. The upper line of exercise No.1-R is the melody. *(Small notes.)* The lower line of exercise No.1-R *(Large notes)* is the same melody in an improvised form. You will notice that wherever the melody in the upper line is sustained by whole notes, *(See Measures 3 and 4 - 7 and 8 - 10 - 12 - also 1st and 2nd endings.)* A ragtime rhythm has been applied to give a ragtime effect. This idea can always be applied to any selection where the melody is sustained at different places for a measure or more. When you come to these sustained parts of the melody, instead of applying a ROLL to sustain, apply a ragtime rhythm instead. Study this exercise carefully and you will soon get the idea of this.

1-R. Practice several times and Keep a steady tempo. Memorize both lines.

The following exercise *(no. 2-R)* is based upon the same melody as above *(Ex. No.1-R Upper line)* but has been improvised in an entirely different manner. You will notice that in measures No. 3 and 4 - 7 and 8 - 10 - 12 and in the 1st and 2nd endings, a VARIATION effect has been applied instead of a Ragtime Rhythm. You will also notice that the RAGTIME RHYTHM has been applied to the remaining measures of this exercise, whereas in Exercise 1-R *(Upper line)* these same measures are written in QUARTER NOTES, which is the melody. This idea can be applied to almost any number you play where the melody is occasionaly sustained.

2-R. Repeat several times.

Key of C MAJOR- C TIME *(same as 4/4 time.)* This exercise should be practiced until it can be played at a very fast tempo, and at the same time retaining a STRICT STEADY TEMPO. This exercise MUST BE MEMORIZED. Take one line at a time *(4 measures)* and Keep repeating it until you are able to look down at the instrument and play it from memory at a fast tempo, then take the next line and treat in a similar manner, and so on. After you have thus memorized each line, then play the exercise as written from memory. Practice this exercise until you are able to do this. Keep the hammers LOW and strike the sharps and flats on the ends of the bars.

You will notice that the ROLL on the WHOLE NOTE *(3rd measure of each line)* starts with the LEFT HAND. This is to get you accustomed to always start the ROLL with the LEFT HAND, whenever possible.

LESSON TWENTY-RAGTIME (MELODY FORM)

The following exercise *(no. 4-R)* is to show how the BLUE RHYTHM contained in Exercise **2**-R and **3**-R can be applied to a melody. The upper line *(small notes)* is the melody and the lower line *(large notes.)* is the SAME MELODY, using the BLUE RHYTHM contained in this lesson. This example is to demonstrate how easily you can "RAG UP THE MELODY" by applying these different rhythms. But remember, you must FIRST learn these rhythms before attempting to apply them. After you have thoroughly memorized exercises **1**-R - **2**-R and **3**-R then study this page.

By memorizing the upper line *(melody.)* you will find that the lower line will come much easier. Both the upper and lower lines afford excellent practice therefore, devote all the time possible to them. Keep a steady tempo throughout.

Are you devoting all the time possible to practice? The more you practice the quicker you will gain results.

The Ragtime rhythm contained in the following exercises is in the form of BLUES, and is one of the most commonly used BLUES that can be played on the Xylophone. This BLUE rhythm can be very easily applied to almost any melody written in a major Key. Memorize these exercises thoroughly and keep practicing these rhythms until you can play them absolutely smooth and without stumbling. Strike all double-notes precisely together. After you become familiar with these exercises, COUNT TWO to each measure.

Key of E FLAT MAJOR *(Three Flats)* in **C** time. *(Same as* $\frac{4}{4}$ *time.)* This entire lesson is written in **MAJOR SIXTHS**. Too much importance cannot be given to the practice and study of **DOUBLE - STOPS** *(Double notes)* Double Stops will give a perfect technique quicker than anything else. It is the best material for the pupil to practice. In this lesson, be sure and observe the three flats (B FLAT, E FLAT and A FLAT.) Strike all the flats on the ends of the bars. Keep a steady tempo and count FOUR to each measure. Strike both notes precisely together. Do not attempt to play this lesson TOO FAST. Much more will be gained by playing slow enough so as to be able to strike every note correctly, AT A STEADY TEMPO. This is important.

1. Repeat twenty times without stopping Keep a STEADY TEMPO.

When playing the following exercise, be sure to strike both notes precisely together, Form the habit of doing this whenever you play double-stops *(Double-Notes.)* Always keep a STEADY TEMPO. If your instrument is only 3 octaves, with the note C being the lowest note, play this exercise one octave higher than written. *(Also exercises No. 3 - 4 - 5 - 7 and 8 of this lesson)*

2. Repeat six times without stopping.

In order to develop SPEED when playing these exercises, Keep the hammers LOW, and strike all the sharps and flats on the ends of the bars. Then play as fast as you can IN TEMPO and at the same time, STRIKING EVERY NOTE CORRECTLY. Memorizing these exercises will help you to play them fast and also accurate, as this will enable you to look down at the instrument.

3. Repeat fifteen times without stopping

4. Repeat fifteen times without stopping

5. Repeat fifteen times without stopping notice the COUNT

The following exercise *(No 6)* should be memorized and then practiced until it can be played smooth and without effort. Do not RUSH THE TEMPO. Be sure and give four counts to each measure. In order that you may always strike every note correctly, I suggest the following method. When first playing over any exercise, play it very, very slow and at an absolute steady tempo. Then gradually increase the tempo each time you repeat it. Then keep on increasing the tempo until you are playing as fast as possible without striking any wrong notes. Then STAY AT THIS TEMPO, and continue to practice. Excellent results will be gained by following this method.

When practicing the following exercise *(No 7.)* Roll on every note. Memorize, so that you can look down at the Keyboard. Strike each note with a FIRM ROLL. Better results will be gained this exercise by not attempting to play too fast. In making the jumps from one note to the next, See that no notes in between are struck. Favor a short ROLL on each note

The following exercise *(No 8)* is similar to a chromatic Scale Construction IN SIXTHS. You will find that this exercise can be played faster than most of the others. Memorize, and then look down at the instrument. Keep a steady tempo.

Ragtime- Key of E FLAT MAJOR *(three flats.)* **C** time *(same as 4/4 time.)* The following exercises are to give an idea as to how a melody can be retained throughout IN SIXTHS. Double-stops offer excellent material to practice on, as both hands are taught to work in unison. In exercise No 1-R you will notice that the 4th and 5th notes in each measure are tied together and the two notes are sustained with a ROLL. Make this roll SHORT, otherwise it will be carried into the next note, and the effect of this rhythm will be lost. Wherever a similar construction occurs, this rule holds good.

The following exercise *(No 2-R)* is written in melody form. Memorize, **repeat many times IN TEMPO**, and always play the 1st ending when repeating. Only play the 2nd ending when you decide to stop. Strike all sharps and flats on the ends of the bars. And strike both notes together.

The following exercise *(No 3-R)* contains a trick rhythm that can be used very effectively in many different foms of melody. Memorize this exercise thoroughly, especially the rhythm contained in the 1st and 2nd measures. Roll only where the notes are marked with a roll. Count TWO in each measure. Keep a STEADY TEMPO.

This lesson is written in the Key of C in 2/4 time. The exercises contained herein are in the form of a VARIATION. These exercises, when once memorized, can, with a little practice, be applied to almost any melody. This form of variation is used more than any other, and it is also one of the easiest variations to play. The following exercises, (No. 1A, 2A, 3A, 4A, and 5A) gives the chord, and the variation to fit the chord. This same form of variation can be applied in the same manner to any chord, and in any Key, and the same hammering will prevail. Repeat these exercises many times, until you are thoroughly familiar with this form of variation. Then try them in a different Key. You will find that it is easy, once you have the idea of it. This form of variation can start or stop on any note in the chord, so long as the variation retains the TEMPO.

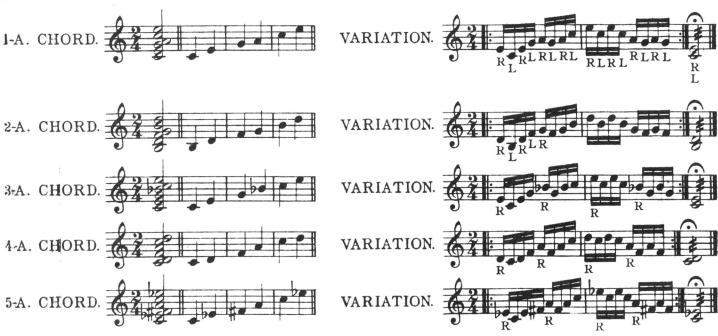

The following exercises (No. 1, 2, 3, 4, and 5) are the same as Exercises No. 1A, 2A, 3A, 4A, and 5A, with the exception that these exercises take in TWO OCTAVES instead of ONE OCTAVE. Practice these exercises until they can be played SMOOTHLY and WITHOUT EFFORT. Strike every note correctly. MEMORIZE. You will find that this form of variation becomes very brilliant and pleasing, when played fast, in tempo, and with every note struck correctly. Practice until you can do this.

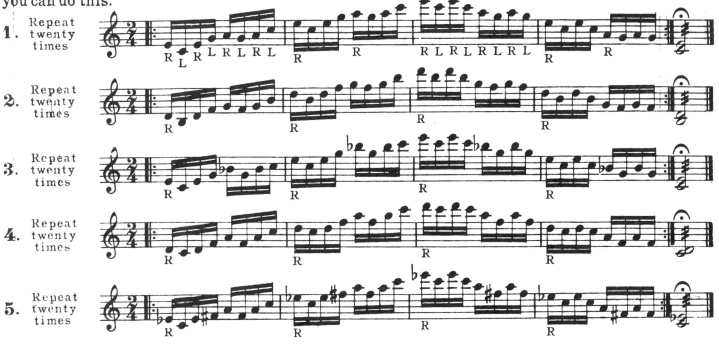

The following exercise (No. 6.) is to show how this form of variation can be applied to a melody. You will note that this exercise is in ¾ time. First, memorize the melody (*UPPER LINE, SMALL NOTES*.) Then memorize the variation, (*LOWER LINE, LARGE NOTES*.) This will give you the idea as to how easily this form of variation will fit a melody. Keep a steady tempo, and strike every note correctly. Practice until you are able to play this variation perfectly smooth.

The following exercise (No. 7.) is constructed the same as above, except that it is inverted or reversed. Instead of the variation form ASCENDING, this variation form DESCENDS. It will harmonize with the melody given above. Play SMOOTH and IN TEMPO. Note the hammering. Each measure begins with the LEFT HAND.

Ragtime - Key of C major, ¢ time (*Play at a Fox-Trot Tempo.*) The exercise given below is an excellent study to develop accuracy in playing Ragtime. This exercise can be made as difficult as the pupil may wish, by simply increasing the tempo. However, always bear in mind the following:- Do not attempt to play so fast that you strike wrong notes. Every note must be struck correctly, and the entire exercise MUST be played IN TEMPO, in order to gain the proper results. Devote all the time possible to this exercise. Strike the double-notes precisely together. Memorize, if possible. Observe the hammering. The hammering is the same throughout the entire exercise.

Key of B Flat Major *(Two flats)* in ¼ time. The following exercise is for the purpose of developing SIGHT-READING. To gain the best results from this exercise, keep a Steady Tempo, slow enough so that EVERY NOTE can be struck correctly, and DO NOT look down at the instrument. Keep your eyes on the music all the time. If you will concentrate on what you are doing, play slow, and look at EVERY NOTE, you will find that SIGHT-READING will soon become easy. When practicing any exercise with the idea of developing sigh-reading, never look down at the instrument. This may seem hard to do at first, but, with practice, you will soon get accustomed to it.

Roll on every note in this exercise. Begin the roll with the LEFT-HAND and end it with the Right. Devote as much practice as possible to this exercise.

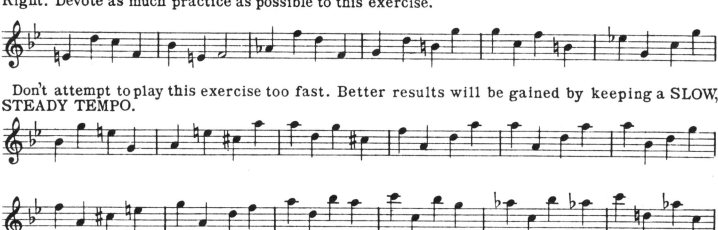

Don't attempt to play this exercise too fast. Better results will be gained by keeping a SLOW, STEADY TEMPO.

LESSON TWENTY-THREE– RAGTIME

The following exercises will give a new idea of ragtime, somewhat similar to SLAP - TONGUE on a Saxophone. To get the best results from these ideas, be sure and ACCENT the notes that are accented, give a sort of SLAP to each accented note, and to the notes that are not accented, play them very soft. This method will give the contrast necessary to produce this SLAP effect. Don't forget, LOUD on the accented notes, and very soft on the others. You will find it very easy, once you get the idea. Keep a steady Tempo. Observe the DOTTED-EIGHTH NOTES.

The following exercises will give an idea as to how this effect can be applied to the ROLL. Play the roll soft and only accent the very last beat in the roll, with the RIGHT-HAND. You will find that the accent usually falls on the RIGHT-HAND whether you are playing a ROLL or SINGLE NOTES.

The following exercise is written in Melody form, and this exercise can be played as a Rag-time Solo. Have an easy piano accompaniment made for this melody, and you can play it either as a Solo or for dancing. If you decide to play it as a solo, memorize it first. And in order to bring out the idea of these accents, do not try to play too fast. Note the accents carefully. Play soft where the notes are not accented. Roll only on the notes marked with a roll.

Note. Play the 1st Strain twice, taking the 1st and 2nd endings. Then play the 2nd strain twice. Then follow the sign ⅜ by going back to first strain and playing once, taking the ending marked, TO TRIO. Play the TRIO twice, and finish with the BREAK.

Key of C Major-in C time - Same as $\frac{4}{4}$ time. This exercise is an excellent study to develop technique and smoothness. This exercise should be memorized, and by memorizing one line at a time, this can be easily done. When the exercise is thoroughly memorized, then look down at the Key-board and work up SPEED. Strike the sharps and flats on the ends of the bars. Strike EVERY NOTE correctly therefore govern the speed accordingly. If necessary, at first, count FOUR to each measure, then when you are more familiar with the exercise, count TWO to each measure. Be sure and give the same count to the 3rd and 4th measures of each line as you do to the 1st and 2nd measures. Each measure MUST receive the same count value. Devote all the time possible to this exercise.

It will be noticed that in exercises Nº 2-3 and 4 there is no hammering marked. Practice these exercises both ways. First by starting with the LEFT HAND, and then by starting with the RIGHT HAND. These exercises are excellent studies to develop SPEED, so memorize them first and then look down at the Key board and play as fast as possible without striking wrong notes.   Keep a steady tempo. Practice each exercise many times.

Use the hammering as explained above. Keep the hammers Low. Play as smooth as possible. Observe the RESTS.

Strike the sharps on the extreme ends of the bars. This will help to give speed. Practice this exercise many times until it can be played very smooth. You may play these exercises as fast as you wish, so long as you strike all notes corretly and keep a steady tempo. Form the habit of doing this whenever you practice, and you will soon notice a big difference in your playing.

Ragtime- Key of C Major - **c** or 4/4 time - Keep a steady tempo and memorize these rhythms. It is always best to practice ragtime exercises at a strict dance tempo*(FOX TROT)*, but until you are familiar with the exercises, play them slow.

The following exercises will give a good idea as to how these rhythms sound when played in the form of a melody. Be sure to strike the double notes together. Don't play the double notes in SEE-SAW fashion, or the rhythm will become uneven. Note the last two measures can be applied as a jazz ending to any 4/4 time melody that ends in the same Key and Chord.

Note. When applying the last two measures of either Exercise 3-R or 4R as a jazz ending to a dance melody, simply substitute them for what ever is contained in the last two measures of the melody. In other words, instead of playing the last two measures of the melody, play these last two measures instead. It is understood, of course, that these endings MUST harmonize with the Key and Chord of the melody.

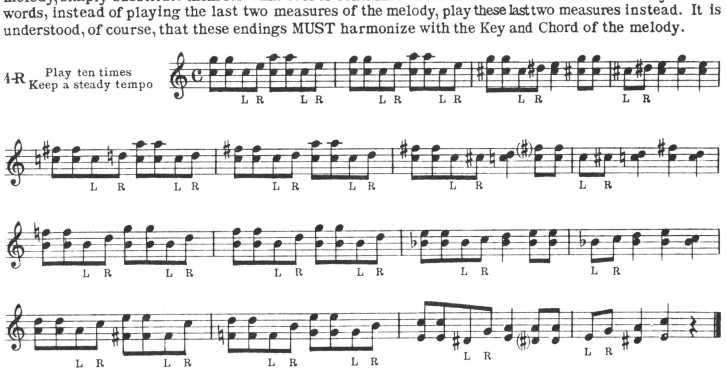

Key of D major *(TWO SHARPS)* in 2/4 TIME. This entire lesson is on a form of variation that can be applied to any chord and in any Key. These exercises MUST be memorized and learned thoroughly, so that later on, when you wish to apply them to a melody, you will have them right under your fingers. In exercise 1, the chord of D major is given, and also the variation to harmonize with the chord. In exercise 1-A, the same variation is given in TWO OCTAVES. In exercise 2 and 2-A, The same chord of D major is given with the variation REVERSED. Practice SLOW AT FIRST until the variation becomes familiar — Strike C# and F# always on the end of the BAR. Remember, NO WRONG NOTES.

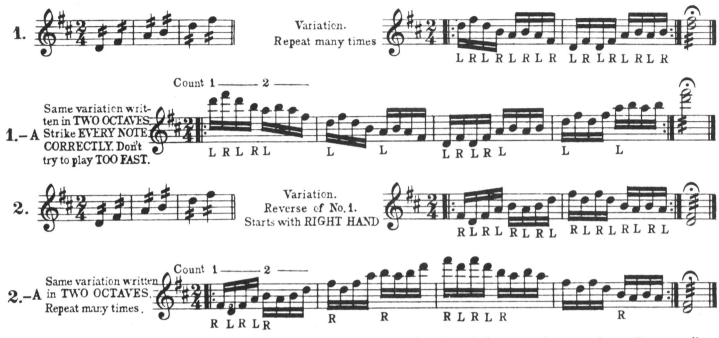

This form of variation can be started from any note in any chord, and the same hammering will prevail. The following exercise, No. 3, will give an idea of this. For example, take the chord of D major Divide exercise No. 3, into four groups of four measures each. The first note in the first group starts on D, which is the first note in the chord, and so on. Practice this exercise many times in tempo, and give FULL COUNT to the measures containing the half notes.

4. The following will give an idea as to how this form of variation will fit ANY CHORD. Simply find the notes in the chord, and then apply this form of variation to the SAME NOTES in the chord. The hammering will always remain the same, whether playing one or two octaves or more. Try this on other chords in other Keys.

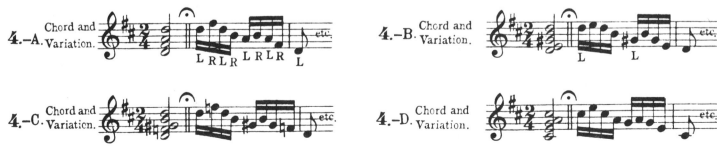

RAGTIME – MELODY FORM

Key of D major *(TWO SHARPS)* in 2/4 TIME. This entire lesson is written in the form of a SOLO, and the same idea given in this lesson as to the form of variation used, prevails throughout. By having a piano accompaniment made to this melody, you will have an excellent ONE STEP SOLO, that can be played either as a SOLO or for Dancing. Memorize the entire number thoroughly. Don't try to play it TOO FAST, as every note must be struck correctly. Note the Routine:— Play the Introduction once, then play the 1st strain twice taking the 1st and 2nd endings, play the SECOND strain twice, taking the 1st and 2nd endings, then D.S. *(note the sign ⅍)* back to the first strain, play it once and take the last ending to TRIO. *(Note change of Key in Trio.)* Play the TRIO twice and finish. Strike all sharps on the ends of the Bars. Practice very slow IN TEMPO until you become familiar with the melody. Then gradually increase SPEED.

Key of E MINOR (*Key of G Signature*) in $\frac{12}{8}$ time. See instructions at beginning of lesson SEVENTEEN regarding MINOR KEYS. Memorize this entire lesson if possible. Play slow at first until you become familiar with the exercises then increase the tempo. Strike every not correctly. Keep the hammers LOW.

Practice the following exercises (*No. 2 and 3*) until they can be played perfectly smooth, in tempo, and from memory. Play them slow at first.

In the following exercise No. 4, Strike both notes exactly together. If you attempt to play this exercise too fast, your arms will become tired. This must be avoided, so govern speed accordingly.

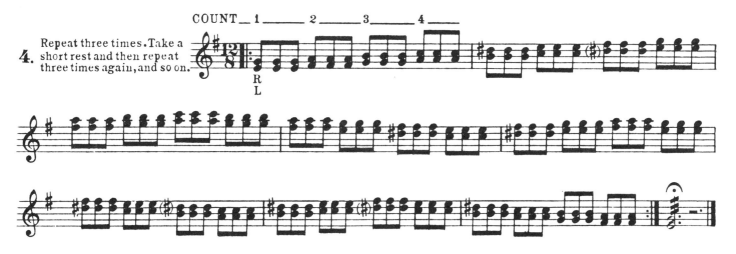

The following exercises (*No. 5 and 6*) are more examples of broken chords. Practice until they can be played thoroughly smooth. Note the hammering in Ex. 6.

The following exercise N⁰ 7. is in melody form, and should be thoroughly memorized. Dont at-tempt to play this exercise too fast. Much more will be gained by playing it slower, and observing a steady tempo throughout. The hammering is the same throughout the entire exercise. Practice many times, and strike each note correctly.

Key of E MINOR *(Key of G SIGNATURE,)* in ¢ time *(Play the same as ⁴/₄ time,)* Practice exercises Nº 1-R and 2-R until you are thoroughly familiar with these rhythms. Always practice these ragtime exercises at a strict dance tempo. Observe the hammering.

The following exercise is in melody form and the rhythms contained herein are the same as in Exercises Nº 1-R and 2-R. This melody should be thoroughly memorized. This exercise will give an idea as to how these rhythms can be used as a melody. Practice many times always at a steady tempo.

Key of F major - (ONE FLAT) in $\frac{4}{4}$ time. When practicing exercise No. 1, count either FOUR to each measure or TWO to each measure. If you practice this exercise very slow, give four counts to each measure. This is an excellent study to develop both technique and sight-reading. The hammering is the same throughout. Repeat the first eight measures each time you play this exercise. Practice very slowly at first and keep a steady tempo. Avoid stumbling as much as possible by playing slow. Devote as much time as possible to this exercise.

This rhythm can be applied to any three note chord in any Key. For example take the first measure in exercise 1-R. The chord here would be an F major chord, the three notes in the chord being F, A and C. To apply this rhythm to this chord of three notes, Strike the two outside notes, which would be F and C, then strike one-half tone below the middle note in the chord, which would be G sharp. Then strike the middle note in the chord, which would be A. This can be done with any chord of three notes. Strike the two outside notes, then a half tone below the middle, then the middle note.

The following exercise is in the form of a melody. Memorize and then repeat many times. Play at about a FOX-TROT Tempo. Play slow at first, so that you will be able to strike every note correctly.

Key of F major - (one flat.) Keep a steady tempo, and practice slow enough so that every note can be struck correctly. Keep the hammers low and strike the sharps and flats on the ends of the bars.

3-R Practice this scale five minutes without stopping

The following exercise (No. 4-R) is written in the form of a melody, and below you will find SIX different endings with which to end this melody. The object of this is to give an idea as to applying a jazz ending to a melody. The usuel ending of a melody like this one would be to sustain the Key note, which is F major, throughout the 15th and 16th measures. (Last two measures) By applying these different endings, the melody can be finished with a jazz effect.

4-R

Memorize this melody first, then all you will have to do will be to watch for the different endings. If you memorize the six different endings, so much the better. Then you can play the melody through SIX times and play a different ending each time. These endings can be used to end nearly any popular melody that you play where the melody ends in the Key of F major. When applying these endings, ALWAYS play the melody first. Don't just practice on the endings, Practice them WITH the MELODY.

Key of C major in 9/8 time. In 9/8 time there are nine eighth-notes to each measure: If necessary, at first count THREE to each measure, then when the exercises become familiar, count ONE to each measure. Memorize this entire lesson, if possible. Strike all double notes together.

1. REPEAT FIFTEEN TIMES

Practice the following exercise very slow at first, so that you are able to go through it the first time, IN TEMPO. If the tempo is slow enough, this can be done.

2. PLAY TEN TIMES

Devote as much time as possible to the following exercises (No 3 and 4,) Double stops (double notes) are the best form of material to practice, as they develop an even touch in both hands, Always strike both notes together.

3. REPEAT TEN TIMES

4. REPEAT SIX TIMES

Memorize this exercise and devote as much time as possible to it. Always play it slow enough so that every note can be struck correctly. In this lesson speed is not necessary.

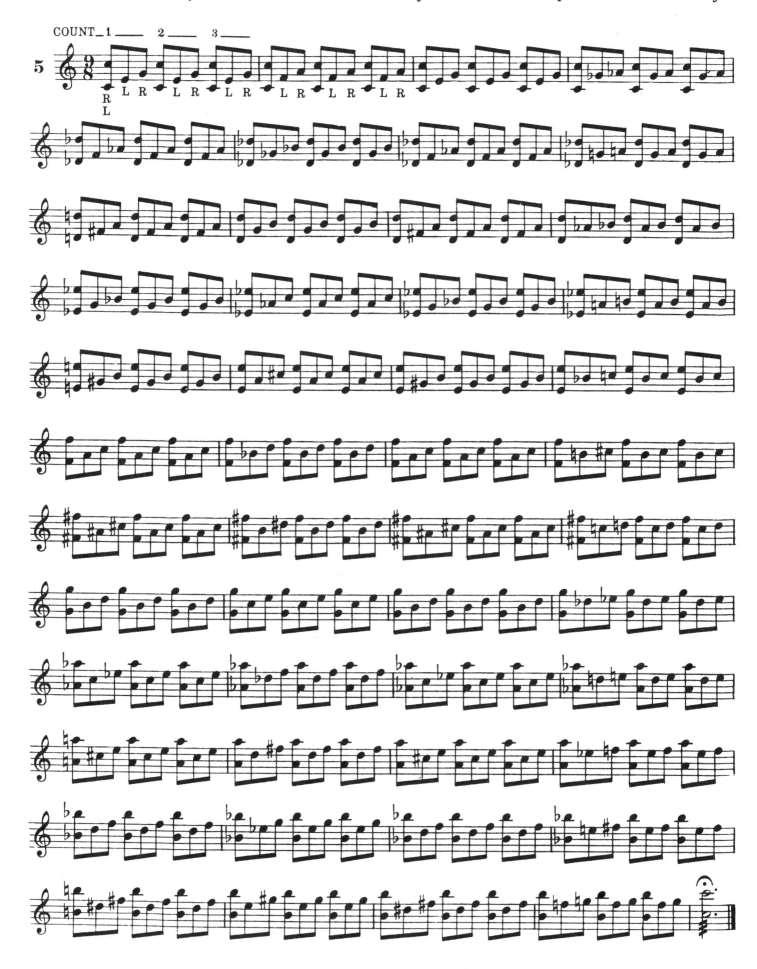

Key of C major in 𝄵 time (play same as 4/4 time.) This rhythm can be applied to any chord of four notes and in any key. This exercise will show how this can be done. The top line (small notes) is the melody and is written in CHORDS. The lower line contains the rhythm to fit the chords. Memorize this exercise. Always take FIRST ENDING to repeat.

1-R Repeat many times, and always repeat IN TEMPO.

LESSON TWENTY-NINE

Key of F major in C time (*Same as 4/4 time.*) Exercise No. 1 is an excellent study to develop sight-reading. Count FOUR to each measure and keep a SLOW STEADY TEMPO. Do not attempt to play this exercise too fast, memorize if possible. When playing this exercise at sight, LOOK entirely at the music. A slow steady tempo will enable you to do this. Devote as much time as possible to practice. ROLL on each note.

The following exercise (No. 1-R) will be frequently found in different ragtime melodies. There are two ways of hammering this exercise and either way is good. Practice both ways. This same ham - mering will hold good in any key. Strike every note correctly, and observe the dotted eighth notes. Keep a steady tempo. Repeat many times.

Exercise No. 2-R shows how double notes may be applied to this rhythm. You will notice that the MEL-ODY of this exercise is all RIGHT HAND. This will necessitate a SLOWER TEMPO.— Repeat many times IN TEMPO. Practice SLOW.

Exercise No. 3-R shows how this rhythm may be played in SYNCOPATED FORM. The melody of this exercise is all RIGHT HAND. This same form of rhythm and hammering will hold good in any key. Prac-tice many times. Not too fast. SLOWER PRACTICE will bring better results. STEADY TEMPO.

Exercise 4-R and 5-R contain a trick rhythm that is used a lot in modern dance melodies. Practice exercise 4-R until the rhythm becomes thoroughly familiar. Exercise 5-R contains the same rhythm in melody form. Memorize this melody. If neccessary memorize four measures at a time. Observe the dotted eighth notes. Whenever you practice dotted eight-notes, practice them SLOW. You will find the rhythm is much better when played SLOW. Keep a STEADY TEMPO.

Key of C major ²⁄₄ time. Exercise No. I should be practiced slow at first until memorized. My reason for advising a very slow tempo at first is that I want the pupil to be able to play the exercise in tempo, all through, and at the same time. striking every note correctly. If the pupil will play slow enough, this can be done the very first time. This method is very beneficial to both sight-reading and developing technique, and I advise all of my pupils to practice everything in this way. You will over come all of your faults by following this method of study. After you have memorized this exercise, then gradually increase the tempo.

The following may be played as a SOLO or for dancing as it is complete, with an introduction and three strains. This will give an idea as to how this BLUE effect is used. Memorize this entire melody.

NOTE: By having an accompaniment made to this melody you can play it either on your dance engagement, or anywhere as a Ragtime Solo.

Key of C major in ¢ time (play the same as 4/4 time.) The following exercise will give a new idea on playing BLUES. In order to get a real BLUE effect, strike the grace-note and the legitimate note (large note) together. This will give a sort of SMEAR effect that is decidely BLUE. Remember, keep a slow drag tempo throughout. BLUES written in Fox-Trot tempo should always be played slow. There is a different style of BLUES which are written in 2/4 time (one step) which are played fast. This will be given later. Practice the following exercises until you are thoroughly familiar with them, as they will give you the idea of this effect.

1-R Repeat twenty times in tempo SLOW

2-R Repeat twenty times.

3-R Repeat twenty times.

The grace-note should always be struck with the RIGHT-HAND.

4-R Repeat twenty times.

5-R

Aways strike the grace-notes that are marked with flats, on the ENDS of the bars.

6-R

7-R

This entire lesson is based on the DIMINISHED CHORD. Look up the definition of a CHORD. INTERVALS, DIMINISHED CHORD, and BROKEN CHORD in a DICTIONARY of Music. Exercise No 1-2-3 and 4 consist of broken chords in DIMINISHED FORM. There is no hammering marked on these exercises. Therefore, practice them BOTH WAYS. Start first with the LEFT HAND and then with the RIGHT HAND. Memorize

Exercise No. 4 should be memorized and then played completely through, IN TEMPO, and without a mistake. This can be done if the tempo is slow enough. Keep a STRICT, STEADY TEMPO throughout. Strike all sharps and flats on the ends of the BARS. When ROLLING on a note containing a sharp or flat, put one hammer on the end of the bar and the other hammer in the middle.

In the following exercise (No. 5) observe the QUARTER NOTE in each measure, give it FULL COUNT. Practice many times IN TEMPO and strike all notes correctly. SLOW AT FIRST. Use both ways to hammer (Practice a while with RIGHT HAND starting and then practice with LEFT HAND starting)

Exercise 6 is a RAGTIME VERSION of exercise 5. The hammering is the same in each measure (exeepting the last two measures.) Dont forget to strike the sharps and flats on the ENDS.- Keep the hammers LOW.

Exercise No. 7 is in melody form and will show the difference between the MAJOR CHORDS (1st and 2nd measures) and diminished chords (3rd and 4th measures) and so on. Memorize and strike every note correctly. PLAY SLOW AT FIRST.

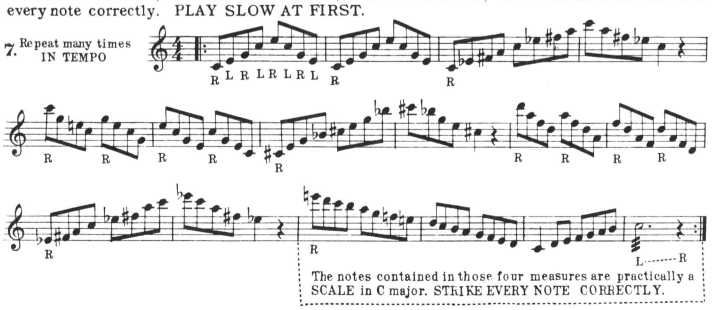

The notes contained in those four measures are practically a SCALE in C major. STRIKE EVERY NOTE CORRECTLY.

Key of C major($\frac{4}{4}$ time) and based on DIMINISHED CHORDS. Practice many times. SLOW AT FIRST, memorize if possible. Count either TWO or FOUR to each measure. You will no_ tice that from the 33rd measure on, the construction changes. The chord is started from the TOP with the RIGHT HAND. This change MUST BE MADE IN TEMPO.   DO NOT STOP when going from the 32nd measure into the 33rd measure.

Key of E flat major in **4/4** time. Exercise No. 1 is an excellent study to develop the LEFT HAND. Count four to each measure. The hammering remains the same throughout the entire exercise — Strike all sharps and flats on the ends of the bars. Do not attempt to play this exercise too fast, as speed is not necessary in this exercise. Keep a steady tempo and strike every note correctly. Keep the hammers LOW. Memorize, if possible, and then practice without the music.

1 — Practice many times each day. Always in tempo note the hammering.

Key of E flat major - in ¢ time (play the same as 4/4 time.) This lesson will give an idea as to how a melody can be followed with a ragtime rhythm. First practice Exercise 1-R until this rhythm can be played at a strict fox-trot tempo from memory.

Exercise 2-R contains a melody (top line, small notes) and a ragtime version of the same melody. Any melody similar to this one can be featured in the same way. Simply follow the melody, and instead of playing it straight, as written, play it with a ragtime rhythm. Exercise 2-R will give a good example of this method of "RAGGING" a melody.

Exercise 3-R will give an idea as to how a different rhythm can be applied to the same melody. This rhythm is excellent to feature throughout an entire strain, as it is somewhat different than the usual ragtime.This rhythm can be applied to practically any melody, and in any Key, by following the melody and playing it in the form of this rhythm.

The following exercise- (No. 4-R) will fit the melody given in Exercise No.2-R.(TOP LINE.) This will show how the entire melody can be featured by applying this rhythm. Practically any melody can be featured in the same way.

The best way to develop a good ragtime technique is to continually practice these different exercises. Even when you think that you have mastered these different rhythms, continue to practice them. Continually going over them is what will bring results.

Key of G-major-in ¢ time.(play the same as 4/4 time.) Exercise No. 1 contains a melody (verse and chorus) that is similar to the average Fox Trot that is played for dancing. This lesson is to show how the average dance number can be played by featuring ragtime rhythms, etc.   Regarding improvising in a dance melody:— First, play the straight melody AS WRITTEN in order to get an idea as to what the melody is like. It is much easier to improvise if you KNOW THE MELODY.   Therefore practice Exercise No. 1 until you are thoroughly familiar with it, and can play it from memory. By doing this, you will be able to play the ragtime version of it much easier. Keep a steady tempo and count TWO to each measure. Play Exercise 1 exactly as written.

Practice this melody many times each day. After it becomes too easy, increase tempo. Strike every note correctly. Keep the hammers low. Remember, the verse is just as important as the chorus, so devote your practice accordingly.

Exercise No. 2 is a ragtime version of the melody contained in Exercise No. 1. If you have thoroughly memorized Exercise No. 1. you will readily see how this melody is played in Ragtime form. Always remember, when "RAGGING" a melody, you MUST be able to distinquish the melody AT ALL TIMES. You will notice how the melody has been carried throughout. No matter what melody you may want to play in ragtime form, DON'T LOSE THE MELODY. This is important. Practice Exercise 2 until you have a thorough idea as to how the melody is carried in Ragtime Form.

*) NOTE — In measures that contain whole notes, it is well to feature a figure or scale form, (see measures 3 and 4, and also 15. in the VERSE.) In these measures you will notice that the melody is retained in the first note (quarter note) of each measure. This leaves the remainder of the measure in which to improvise a figure or scale form of some sort. This, of course, must be done, IN TEMPO.

Exercise No. 3 will show how a different rhythm can be applied to this chorus. This rhythm is somewhat similar to an accompaniment and therefore may be played throughout the entire chorus without the rhythm being changed. It will be noticed, however, that the MELODY is still in evidence. To apply this rhythm to any melody, simply play the melody in this rhythm. All that is necessary is to thoroughly learn this rhythm, then play it through the entire strain, and follow the melody.

Exercise No. 4 is another rhythm that can be applied to this chorus. It may be necessary to play this rhythm SLOWER, on account of the DOUBLE NOTES. You will note that the melody is followed and retained throughout. ROLL only on the notes so marked.

Keep a steady tempo, Strike both notes precisely together.

Key of F major in 𝄴 time (same as $\frac{4}{4}$ time.) Exercise No 1 is an excellent study to develop the right-hand. DO NOT attempt to play this exercise too fast. Keep a steady tempo and strike EVERY NOTE CORRECTLY. This can be done by playing SLOW memorize, if possible.

EXERCISE No. 1-R contains a verse and chorus that is similar to the average Fox-Trot melody played for dancing. Practice this melody until it can be played perfectly IN TEMPO. Play it just as it is written. It is very important that the pupil becomes proficient in playing a STRAIGHT MELODY as well as a RAGTIME MELODY. Memorize this entire exercise and be sure that the tempo remains steady throughout. Accustom yourself to playing these melodies exactly as they are written. Count TWO to each measure. This melody should be memorized first, before attempting to play Exercise 2-R

Are you striking the sharps and flats on the ENDS of the BARS? Practice this exercise many times each day. This will develop SMOOTHNESS in your playing.

EXERCISE No. 2-R is a ragtime version of the melody contained Exercise No. 1-R you will notice that the melody is still in evidence. In ragging a melody, you must be able to distinguish the melody AT ALL TIMES. NEVER LOSE THE MELODY. This exercise is another example as to how a melody may be carried in the form of ragtime. Practice this exercise as much as possible.

You will note that in the CHORUS, the 1st and 2nd measures, which contain the MOTION of the melody (see Exercise no. 1-R, chorus.) a ragtime rhythm has been applied. In the 3rd and 4th measures, where the melody is sustained (see 3rd and 4th measures of Ex. 1-R, chorus.) a variation form has been applied. The same system prevails throughout the entire chorus. This system may be applied to nearly any melody that is somewhat similar in construction to Exercise No. 1-R. I suggest that the pupil take several dance melodies, in any Key, and follow this system. Apply ragtime rhythms to the MOTION of the melody and apply VARIATION FORMS to the SUSTAINED Part of the melody. Remember, your ragtime and variations MUST harmonize with the melody.

LESSON THIRTY-FIVE

Key of A FLAT MAJOR *(Four Flats)* in 4/4 time. The following exercises *(No. 1-2-3-4-5 and 6)* should be practiced slow enough at first so that EVERY NOTE may be struck correctly, and IN TEMPO. Memorize, if you wish, and then play from memory.

1. Repeat 20 times always in tempo. Note the hammering. This exercise is to develop the LEFT HAND.

2. Repeat 20 times, in tempo. Note the hammering. This exercise is to develop the RIGHT HAND.

3. Repeat 20 times, in tempo. Practice slow enough so that every note can be struck correctly.

4. Repeat 20 times, in tempo. Note the hammering.

5. Repeat 20 times, in tempo. Strike every note correctly.

6. Repeat 20 times, in tempo. Note the hammering.

Key of A FLAT MAJOR *(Four Flats)* in ¢ time *(Play the same as* **4/4** *time.)* In this lesson, a ragtime rhythm is given with the QUARTER NOTE coming FIRST. This gives a very good effect, and practically any rhythm can be played this way.

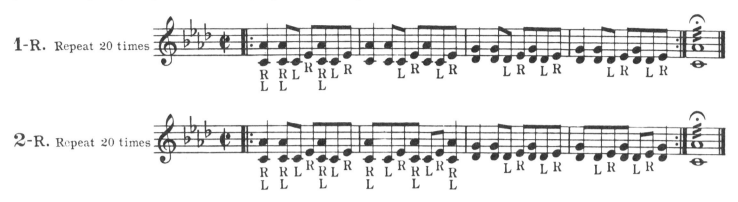

Exercise No. 3-R contains a melody containing the ragtime rhythm with the quarter note coming FIRST. Practice Exercises No. 1-R and 2-R until this rhythm can be played absolutely smooth and IN STRICT TEMPO. Memorize Exercise No. 3-R. Strike every note correctly. Always take the 1st ending to repeat, and always repeat IN TEMPO.

Exercises 4-R, 5-R and 6-R will give an idea as to how the quarter notes can be used throughout an entire measure. Practice and memorize Exercises No. 4-R and 5-R until you are thoroughly acquainted with the rhythm.

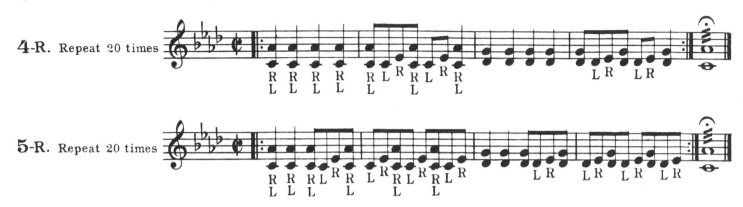

Exercise No. 6-R contains the same melody as Exercise No. 3-R with the exception that the quarter-notes are used throughout an entire measure. These rhythms should be thoroughly memorized. A good form of practice is to try these rhythms on different chords in different Keys. But first learn the rhythms as they are in these exercises.

This entire lesson is based upon a chromatic scale in DOUBLE STOPS (Double Notes.) Exercise No.1 is in MINOR THIRDS. These exercises should be memorized, and practiced until they can be played in strict tempo and absolutely smooth. Start very SLOW so that every note can be struck correctly the first time you play these exercises. If you start SLOW ENOUGH, this can be done. Then gradually increase the tempo.

Exercise No. 2 is in FOURTHS. My reason for advising SLOW PRACTICE is that by practicing slow at first, the pupil is able to HEAR the melody of the exercise CORRECTLY, THE FIRST TIME HE PLAYS IT. All practice and study should be treated in a similar manner.

Exercise No.3 is in MINOR SIXTHS. Do not attempt to play these exercises FAST until after you have memorized them and can play them perfectly at a slow tempo. Then gradually work up speed.

Exercises No. 4, 5 and 6 contain the straight chromatic scales in MINOR THIRDS, FOURTHS and MINOR SIXTHS. Memorize each exercise. Strike each note correctly. Repeat each exercise many times before going to the next.

The following is in the form of a melody (verse and chorus.) and is to give an idea as to how chromatic double-stops may be used as a melody. Memorize first, by playing SLOW. This will enable you to hear the melody CORRECTLY. You will memorize much quicker by doing this. Then work up speed until this melody can be played at a strict Fox Trot tempo. Devote as much time as possible to this melody. Always take the 1st ending of the chorus to repeat. Only take the 2nd ending to finish.

By having an accompaniment made to this melody, it can be played on your engagements; either as a ragtime solo or for dancing.

Exercise No. 1-R is in MINOR THIRDS, IN RAGTIME. Memorize and keep a steady tempo when practicing. If you have thoroughly mastered exercise No. 1, this exercise will not prove difficult. Count either TWO or FOUR to each measure.

Exercise No. 2-R is in FOURTHS, IN RAGTIME. The hammering remains the same throughout each measure in these exercises. Do not forget to practice SLOW AT FIRST. This is the quickest way in which to develop speed.

Exercise No. 3-R is in MINOR SIXTHS, IN RAGTIME. The more time you devote to the LEGITI-MATE FORM OF THESE EXERCISES, as in No. 1-2-3-4-5 and 6, the better you will play them in RAG TIME.

When playing double stops, both notes MUST be struck precisely together. In this lesson, where the exercises are all chromatic, ALL SHARPS AND FLATS MUST be struck on the ends of the bars This will permit you to work up SPEED, and at the same time ACCURACY. If you attempt to go to middle of the bars on the sharps and flats, you will be compelled to use a lot of un-necessary arm movement, which will prove very detrimental to your playing. After you complete this lesson, continue to practice exercises No. 4-5 and 6 for several weeks to come. A few minutes each day spent on these exercises will eventually give a perfect technique on chromatic Double Stops. Keep at them every day. Don't forget to keep your hammers LOW.

Key of G major (one sharp) in ₵ time (play same as 4/4 time.) Exercise No.1. is to give an idea as to the use of TRIPLETS and DOTTED EIGHTH NOTES played in the same melody. This exercise is in the form of a melody, and the pupil should memorize it, and then play it without looking at the music. Count either TWO or FOUR to each measure. Strike every note correctly, and be sure that the correct TIME-VALUE is given to each measure. This exercise may be used as a SOLO, if the pupil cares to have a piano accompaniment made to it. Devote plenty of time to it and learn to play it absolutely SMOOTH, and with no mistakes. Note the change of KEY at the 2nd strain and trio.

NOTE:- The pupil must become accustomed to always observing repeat signs, D.C., D.S., 𝄋 etc.

D.S. is an abbreviation for DAL SEGNO, and means to go back and repeat from the place marked by the sign (𝄋) to the word FINE, or double-bar with a HOLD 𝄐 The letters D.C. are an abbreviation of DA CAPO, which means to go back to the beginning and stop at the double bar with the word FINE, and also marked with a HOLD (𝄐) Therefore, practice this exercise as follows:-
Play the 1st strain TWICE, then the 2nd strain TWICE, then D.S. back to 𝄋, Play the 1st strain ONCE, taking the 2nd ENDING. Play the TRIO TWICE, then D.C. back to beginning, play the 1st strain ONCE, taking 2nd ENDING and FINISH.

Ragtime Key of G major- Exercise No. 1-R contains a melody in the form of STOP-TIME. The lower line of this exercise contains a VARIATION to fit this melody. This variation features TRIPLETS and DOTTED EIGHTH-NOTES throughout. A combination of triplets and dotted eighth-notes gives one of the best forms of variation. It is not necessary that the triplet comes ahead of the dotted eighth-notes. It may be used anywhere in the measure, so long as it harmonizes with the melody. Remember, a variation must ALWAYS be in tempo. Just striking many notes at random, at a fast tempo, is NOT A VARIATION. Memorize the melody first (TOP LINE.) Then work on the variation. Practice until the variation can be played SMOOTHLY, IN TEMPO and with every note struck correctly.

Do not try to play this variation TOO FAST. The word "VARIATION" does not mean "SPEED'

Exercises 2-R, 3-R, and 4-R will give an idea as to how TRIPLETS may be used in con-nection with double note ragtime rhythms. As stated before, TRIPLETS give excellent ragtime and variation effects, when used in connection with other notes. Exercises No. 2-R and 3-R will give the rhythm. Practice these exercises until these rhythms can be played very smooth and in strict tempo.

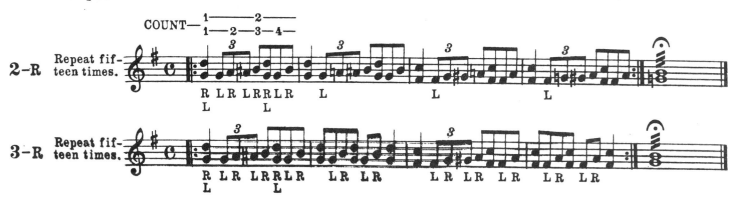

Exercise No. 4-R contains the same STOP-TIME melody that is in Exercise No. 1-R, (TOP LINE) This is a ragtime version of the STOP TIME melody, with the above ragtime rhythm used throughout. These melodies are written so as to conform as near as possible to the average fox-trot chorus. Memorize Exercise 4-R and play it in strict tempo.

DO NOT ATTEMPT TO PLAY TOO FAST

In this lesson, a variation form is given in ALL MAJOR KEYS, in order that the pupil may become aquainted with this form of variation in the major keys. In music, there are TWELVE MAJOR KEYS, and these are given in this lesson.

Always remember, whatever key you are playing in, you MUST always observe the sharps or flats that are contained in the keys. For example, if you are playing in the key of A MAJOR, which contains three sharps, you must always play the notes F, C and G, as F sharp, C sharp and G sharp, unless one of these notes is written with a NATURAL (♮) or a FLAT (♭) in front of it. This rule applies to every key. Whatever the signature of the key is, the sharps or flats contained therein, MUST ALWAYS BE OBSERVED, unless otherwise written.

Practice each exercise in this lesson until you can play this variation form in every major key. Memorize each exercise. DONT try to play them too fast. Every note MUST be struck correctly, therefore play slow enough so as to be able to do this. Repeat each exercise at least twenty times, IN TEMPO.

ARE YOU STRIKING THE SHARPS AND FLATS on the ENDS of the BARS?

8. Key of D FLAT MAJOR (FIVE FLATS)

9. Key of A FLAT MAJOR (FOUR FLATS)

10. Key of E FLAT MAJOR (THREE FLATS)

11. Key of B FLAT MAJOR (TWO FLATS)

12. Key of F MAJOR (ONE FLAT)

Exercises 13, 14 and 15 contain this variation in a diminished form. (*SEE LESSON THIRTY-ONE which is based on the diminished chord.*) Memorize each one thoroughly. It will be noticed that the same hammering prevails throughout regardless of what key this variation is written in.

13. Repeat twenty times

14. Repeat twenty times

15. Repeat twenty times

NOTE: Whenever the word "VARIATION" is mentioned, the general idea seems to be that it is something that should be played VERY FAST. This is a wrong idea that many musicians have. A variation may be played very effectively SLOW as well as FAST.

Key of E FLAT MAJOR - in ¾ time. The variation form given in this melody will give an idea as to how it may be used as a melody, as well as a variation. Memorize, and strike every note correctly. By having a piano accompaniment made to this melody, it may be played either as a waltz for dancing, or as a solo.

Be sure that you give the proper time value to each measure. The same count that you give to the measures containing the sixteenth notes must be given to the measures containing the quarter-notes, dotted half-notes, etc.

LESSON THIRTY-NINE

Key of D Major – in ⁶⁄₈ time.   In the Key of D Major, always observe F sharp and C sharp, unless written otherwise. This lesson will prove very beneficial to the rendition of melodies and especially MARCHES, written in ⁶⁄₈ time. Practice each exercise until it can be played perfectly in tempo and with every note struck correctly If necessay, the pupil may count SIX to each measure in order to work out a steady tempo. Then, when the exercise becomes familiar, count TWO to each measure. Repeat Exercise N⁰ 1 many times

1.

Do not attempt to practice these exercises TOO FAST. Speed can only be acquired by SLOW PRACTICE AT A STEADY TEMPO, in order that each note may be given the proper time-value, and also struck correctly. If this is followed, SPEED will come.

2.

Are you keeping a strict, steady tempo in all practice? If you strike wrong notes, or if you STUMBLE in these exercises, you are playing TOO FAST. Slow down the tempo.

3.

Practice these exercises until they can be played perfectly smooth. Always repeat them IN TEMPO. Memorize each one, and then practice by looking down at the Key board.

4.

Are you striking the SHARPS on the ends of the bars? Are you striking all double-notes precisely together? Are you keeping a STEADY TEMPO?

5. Note the hammering -
The first eight measures are all
for the RIGHT-HAND, and the last
eight measures are all LEFT HAND.

Exercise Nº 6, if practiced diligently, will prove very beneficial in developing the pupil's ability to play 6/8 march melodies. If possible, memoize this exercise. And remember, DON'T attempt to play TOO FAST. Work out each measure IN TEMPO, and with every note struck correctly. This exercise should be practiced until it can be played ALL THE WAY THROUGH in strict tempo. Devote all the time possible to practice.

If this exercise seems too difficult, go back and try it again at a VERY SLOW TEMPO.

The following exercise, No. 1-M, is in melody form, and is similar to the average $\frac{6}{8}$ march. Memorize, and observe all repeats, etc. Devote as much practice as possible to this exercise, as it will give an idea as to the rendition of $\frac{6}{8}$ marches. *(note.)* Never attempt to "RAG UP" a $\frac{6}{8}$ march. Always play $\frac{6}{8}$ marches JUST AS THEY ARE WRITTEN. Save the ragtime for dance melodies written in FOX TROT TEMPO.

(note) - 8va⋯ means to play ONE OCTAVE higher than written. Therefore, after observing the D. S. sign, play the TRIO the last time, one octave higher than written.

Key of C MAJOR – in C time (same as $\frac{4}{4}$ time.) in sixteenth notes. The object of this lesson is to develop the straight variation idea when played together with chromatic scales, straight major scales, etc. Exercise No. 1 contains the variation form with a chromatic form. This exercise MUST be practicd until it can be played very smooth and with EVERY NOTE struck correctly. DON'T try and play too fast. Practice SLOW at first and work out each measure correctly. Count either TWO or FOUR to each measure.

Exercise No. 2 contains the variation form with the straight scale form. Follow the advice given above. Practice many times. Memorize if possible, and then play from memory– Keep a firm, steady tempo, and not TOO FAST.

IMPORTANT:– Variations are easily learned and played, providing the pupil will go about it in the RIGHT WAY. You MUST play slow enough so as to be able to strike every note correctly. If I were standing over you, teaching you, I would make you do this. Many pupils having a bad habit of just speeding through these exercises, and striking everything at random. This is a waste of time, and I do not want any of my pupils to do this. You MUST follow my advice on this, if if you wish to develop a smooth technique.

Practice many times always **3** in tempo. Play from memory, if possible.

Ragtime – Key of C. Exercise No. 1-R is to give an idea of the variation form used in connection with ragtime rhythms – This exercise is similar to a Fox-Trot chorus. You will note that the variation form is in TRIPLETS– A variation in TRIPLETS is usually the best form to apply to the average DANCE MELODY. Examples of this kind will help you to improvise, because, if you devote enough time to these exercises, you will begin to play all popular melodies in a similar manner. Practice this exercise, SLOW AT FIRST, and always in tempo. Then gradually increase the tempo, and play from memory. Then devote many hours to it. Even after you think you have it perfect, Keep at it. This system will develop you quicker than any other.

Key of F major — in ¾ time. The object of this lesson is to give ideas as to the better rendition of sustained melodies. The general idea seems to be that whenever a sustained or SLOW part of a melody is played, especially in dance music, it becomes necessary to FILL IN a lot of arpeggios, breaks, etc. This is a WRONG IDEA. Variations, etc., are very good when they are featured properly, and at the right time during the melody, but when a sustained melody is to be featured, some very beautiful effects can be had by featuring in a SUSTAINED manner. Here is one excellent effect that can be gotten by featuring a three note chord effect throughout. Note the example below:—

A three note chord as it is written.   How it may be played with TWO HAMMERS.

Take the bottom note of the chord, strike it once, similar to a grace note, and run it right into the ROLL on the two top notes. Thus you will get the effect of the three note harmony. This system can be applied to any three note chord in any Key. When written out, this idea would appear like this:—

Always be sure that the bottom note of the chord, which in this idea is the grace-note, is ALWAYS STRUCK CORRECTLY. This is important, otherwise a DISCORD will result. Practice the lower line of Exercise No. 1 many times until the grace note can be worked into the roll absolutely smooth.

Another very good effect that may be had with any sustained melody, and particularly a slow waltz melody, is the SLUR EFFECT, which is similar to the idea of a HAWAIIAN STEEL GUITAR. This idea is very effective for all sustained melodies, and especially when played on the LOWER register of the instrument with SOFT HAMMERS. Example 1-A will show how this slur effect may be applied.

The idea of this effect is to play the three grace notes the same speed as the ROLL, and run them right into the roll of the melody note *(LARGE NOTE)*. It will be noticed that in the fourth measure, the slur DECENDS. This is usually done because the MELODY-NOTE decends, and the idea being to SLUR DOWN TO IT. You may either slur UP or DOWN to a note. If the melody goes up, slur up to it, and if it goes down, slur down to it, etc. It will be noticed that in the seventh measure, the slur contains FOUR NOTES. Occasionally you may use a four note slur, but stick to the THREE NOTE SLUR as much as possible, as it is more effective. When the melody contains QUARTER-NOTES and HALF-NOTES, as in Exercise 2-A. Use the slur on the long notes *(HALF-NOTES)*. DON'T overdo this idea by trying to slur EVERY NOTE. These exercises should be practiced until they can be played very smooth and at a STRICT WALTZ TEMPO. Be sure and play the slurs as smooth as possible.

Exercise No. 3-A will give an idea of the decending slur, and also as it is applied to a melody with the quarter-notes coming first in the measure. Practice until these ideas can be played perfectly smooth.

NOTE. Don't try to play the slurs any louder than the
other notes. Keep the same degree of loudness throughout.

The two exercises given on this page are similar to the average waltz melody   Ex. No. 1-M
contains the three note chord effect. You will notice that this effect is ONLY used on the sustained
notes. DON'T try and apply this effect to the quarter-notes and the faster passages. It should only
be done on the sustained part of the melody. Otherwise, the effect will be spoiled by overdoing it.
Practice this exercise until it can be played perfectly smooth, and in strict tempo, then see NOTE
at the bottom of this page.

Exercise 2-M will give an example as to how a popular waltz melody can be played with a
HAWAIIAN EFFECT. Play these melodies SLOW. You will note that the SLUR is only used on
the sustained notes. DON'T try to apply the slur to every note. Only apply it to the sustained notes.
SEE NOTE BELOW.

NOTE. The object of this lesson is to develop these ideas when playing waltz melodies. My advice is this:- after
you have practiced sufficiently on this lesson so that you thoroughly understand these ideas, take FOUR or FIVE
popular waltz melodies (any Key) and learn to play them in the above manner. You can get the three-note harmony
from the Piano part. Practice these melodies along with this lesson. Work out your melodies both with the three-note
chord effect and with the SLUR effect. PLAY SLOW.

In this lesson, I have given the exercises in the form of popular dance melodies (*CHORUSES*). Exercise No. 1 is to benefit the RIGHT - HAND. These examples should be memorized, and then practiced as much as possible, from memory. Practice until you become thoroughly accustomed to these different styles. When playing the average dance melody, you have no choice as to any particular style or way of playing it. You are compelled to play it according to the construction of the melody. Therefore, develop yourself until you are able to use either hand equally well. My idea in this lesson is to give examples that will feature the RIGHT - HAND, then the LEFT - HAND, and then BOTH HANDS TOGETHER. Exercise No. 1 is to benefit the RIGHT - HAND. You will note that the right hand is featured throughout. Practice very slow at first. You should never, at any time, strike a wrong note, when practicing and studying. This is very important and if you play slow enough, you will be able to follow this advice. If you attempt to play FAST and strike several wrong notes, you are only wasting your time.

Exercise No. 2 is for the development of the LEFT-HAND. First go over this example several times, VERY SLOW, and in absolute STRICT TEMPO. This advise MUST BE FOLLOWED. After you are able to play this example all the way through from memory, then gradually increase the tempo. Don't attempt to play these examples TOO FAST, as your arms and wrists will become stiff and tired, and this should never happen when you are playing. You will note that in this example I have given a certain amount of work for the RIGHT-HAND. I do not believe in SINGLE HANDED practice, that is, playing entirely with one hand, and having the other hand remain idle. Far better results will come by using both hands at once and FAVORING the hand that is to be developed. Therefore, strike both double notes together, observe the dotted eighth notes, and keep a steady tempo. The hammering remains the same throughout this exercise.

IMPORTANT:— When practicing these examples, you MUST always take the 1st ending to repeat. If you repeat ten times, take the 1st ending nine times, and then take the 2nd ending the last time to finish. You MUST always repeat in strict tempo. When playing with an orchestra, you will always be compelled to observe the repeats, etc, in strict tempo, therefore, it is imperative that you train yourself to do this.

Examples No. 3 and 4 contain good material to develop an even stroke with both hands. Follow the same instructions give before in this lesson, namely, SLOW TEMPO at FIRST, STRIKE ALL NOTES CORRECTLY, MEMORIZE, and repeat many times in TEMPO.

3- Always take the 1st ending to repeat.

In Example No. 4, strike all double notes absolutely together. Strike all Sharps and Flats on the ENDS of the bars. The same hammering prevails throughout.

4- Keep the hammers LOW.

In this lesson, the RIGHT HAND is featured in a way that brings out a good ragtime rhythm, and yet, is very easy to play. The four exercises given in this lesson are similar to the average fox-trot chorus. I have found, from experience, that if the pupil devotes sufficient practice and study to exercises written in melody form; then he will begin to play all other melodies along these lines.

The rhythm contained in Exercise No. 1 is the same throughout. Memorize this exercise so that you can play it completely through without looking at the music. Then, after you have it completely memorized, practice several times each day from memory. DON'T think that after you are just about able to get through an exercise, you are then ready for the next lesson. This is a wrong idea. After you practice until you can just about get through an exercise without any mistakes, then you should continue to practice this SAME EXERCISE several hundred times. This plan may entail hard work, but it will surely bring results. Try it and see.

After you are able to play Exercise No. 1 in tempo from memory, then practice it in the rhythm contained below, in Exercise No. 1 A. This will give a different rhythm. Instead of the quarter notes in the beginning of each measure, use a TRIPLET. Exercise No. 1-A will give the idea. Then play the entire exercise No. 1 with this rhythm.

The idea of these rhythms is that the RIGHT-HAND takes two notes in succession. This is really the only difference in this idea of rhythm. Once you get the idea of this rhythm, it becomes very easy to play. Remember what I stated about practicing. After you get so that you can just about play through these exercises without any mistakes, DON'T STOP PRACTIC-ING. Continue to practice for several hundred times. By doing this you will acquire these rhythms so thoroughly that you will be able to apply them to any melody that you play. This is the surest way in which you will develop a real good technique.

Exercise No. 2 is written in the key of A FLAT (FOUR FLATS.) In this exercise, the same right hand idea is featured in connection with a TRIPLET. Memorize and then practice from memory. Be sure that EVERY NOTE is struck CORRECTLY. If these exercises seem diffi-cult at first, practice VERY SLOW until you are able to play all the way through at a VERY SLOW TEMPO. Then gradually increase the tempo. DON'T FORGET, no wrong notes, and al-ways keep a strict, steady tempo. Strike all sharps and flats on the ENDS of the bars.

Exercise No. 3 contains the same right-hand idea, with the exception that the first two notes in each measure are QUARTER-NOTES. Be sure and note that each exercise is written in a different key. Exercise No. 3 is written in the key of D (TWO SHARPS.) Memorize, then repeat from ten to twenty times, IN TEMPO. Always take the FIRST ENDING to repeat. Take the LAST ENDING only to finish.

Exercise No. 4 contains a TRIPLET in connection with this rhythm for the RIGHT-HAND. Memorize, Practice SLOW at first, and keep a steady tempo. This exercise is written in the key of F (ONE FLAT.) Repeat many times.

The exercises given in this lesson are for the purpose of developing ideas as to the so-called "HOT" playing. One of the best methods to get this effect is to feature an accent with the RIGHT-HAND on the 2nd and 4th quarter beats of each measure. This gives an AFTER-BEAT effect that sounds very good from a rhythm standpoint. Exercise No. 1 gives an example as to featuring the accent with the RIGHT-HAND. Practice this exercise until it can be played perfectly smooth, memorize if possible. Repeat many times, in tempo. Repeat from ten to twenty times.

Exercise No. 1-A contains a variation to the melody in Ex. 1. It will be noticed that the accent is always with the RIGHT-HAND, and on the 2nd and 4th quarter beats in the measure. Memorize this exercise, then practice by repeating from ten to twenty times, ALWAYS IN TEMPO.

In this style of playing, it is permissable to feature a triplet, ANYWHERE IN THE MEASURE. The only thing to bear in mind is this:— always keep the accent on the 2nd and 4th quarter beats in the measure. Practice Ex. 1-B until it can be played from memory, then play from memory.

Examples No. 1-C, 1-D, 1-E and 1-F are to show how this melody may be played in several different ways. The accent always remains the same, namely on the 2nd and 4th quarter beats in the measure. When you have learned to play Ex. 1 in these different ways, try to play it by making up your own ideas. Follow the routine outlined here.

Exercise No. 2 is in melody form, similar to a popular dance melody *(CHORUS)*. It will be noticed that the **accents** always remain the same throughout, namely on the 2nd and 4th quarter beats in the measure. Memorize this exercise, then practice every day from memory. When practicing, repeat many times, in tempo. It will be noticed that these exercises are written in different keys.

It is important that you MUST repeat these exercises from ten to twenty times without stopping. Playing them through ONLY ONCE WILL NOT do you any good. You MUST repeat them many times, in order to become able to play these rhythms smooth and without effort.

Exercise No. 4. in the Key of G major. The rhythm is the same and the accents are the same, but the melody is different. The idea of these different melodies in different Keys is to get the pupil accustomed to playing these rhythms in different Keys and still retain the original idea as to accents, etc. Memorize, then practice with many repeats. Strike all notes correctly. These exercises should not be played faster than a good fox-trot dance rhythm.

Ex.- 4   Note the accents.

Exercise No. 5 is in the Key of F major. Memorize, then practice several days from memory, always making the repeats. DON'T strike the accented notes TOO HARD. Just a slight accent is sufficient.

Ex.- 5   Note the accents.

In this lesson, ideas are given pertaining to BLUES. The easiest method of applying BLUES to any melody is as follows: First play the melody in DOUBLE NOTES. (The top note being the melody and the lower note harmonizing.) Then to play the same melody in BLUE form, drop the harmony note a half tone LOWER than it is written, then COME BACK to the ORIGINAL HARMONY NOTE. This will give a BLUE EFFECT to any melody and in ANY KEY. The easiest way to understand this idea is through examples. Therefore, Exercise No. 1 contains a straight melody in DOUBLE NOTES. The upper note is the melody, and the lower note harmonizes. It is important that you learn this melody by MEMORY. Then you will more easily understand the examples that follow.

Be sure and practice Exercise No. 1 until it can be played from memory. Then go to Exercise No. 2. You will notice in Ex. No. 2 that the SAME MELODY prevails, but the harmony note (LOWER NOTE) has been lowered a HALF TONE and then BROUGHT BACK to the ORIGINAL HARMONY NOTE. The idea of alternating from the original harmony note, then a half of a tone FLAT, then back to the original note, etc., is what gives the BLUE effect. Back and forth from the FLAT note to the ORIGINAL note is the proper BLUE EFFECT. This idea may be applied to any melody, and in any Key. Practise and study Exercises No. 1 and 2 until you thoroughly grasp this idea. Dont pass up these two exercise because they may seem too EASY. Practice and repeat them many times each day, in strict tempo.

Exercise No. 3 is a ragtime version of the melody contained in Ex. No. 1. It will be noticed that the alternating idea on the harmony note (LOWER NOTE) is still in evidence. Once you acquire this BLUE IDEA, you may apply it to any ragtime rhythm that you know, and by lowering the harmony note and then coming back to the original harmony note, and then continuing this alternating process, you will be able to play blues in any ragtime rhythm that you wish. Practice and learn from memory, Exercise No. 3. Then play these three exercises over many times each day. In this way, you will acquire this idea of BLUES quickly.

Exercise No. 4 contains a melody in a somewhat different form. Exercise No. 5 contains a ragtime and blue version of the same melody. Practice and study Ex. No. 4 until it can be played all the way through, in strict tempo and from MEMORY. It is very important that you follow this advice and devote plenty of study and practice to these STRAIGHT MELODIES. Otherwise, you will not be able to compare the straight melody with the ragtime version. Practice Exercise No. 4 whether it appears SIMPLE or not. Repeat many times. Always take the 1st ending to repeat. Take the 2nd ending to finish.

Exercise No. 5 contains a ragtime and blue version of Ex. No. 4. As stated before, blues may be played in ANY RAGTIME RHYTHM, by applying the advice given in this lesson. Practice and repeat this exercise many times. Play very slow at first, then gradually increase the tempo Strike the sharps and flats on the ends of the bars. Keep the hammers low.

Exercise No. 6 contains BLUES in DOTTED EIGHTH NOTE FORM. These examples will show how blues may be played in ANY RHYTHM. The alternating idea of the harmony note is always featured. Practice this exercise many times. Work it up to about a FOX TROT tempo as played for dancing.

Exercise No. 7 gives good material to develop the BLUES idea, when played entirely in double notes. Strike both notes precisely together, play in strict tempo and memorize. Repeat many times without stopping. Dont accent. Play smoothly. Hammers Low.

Exercise No 7-A, 7-B, 7-C and 7-D will show how several different rhythms may be applied to Exercise No. 7. Exercise No 7 must be learned and memorized first of course. Then play the same exercise, all the way through, in the different rhythms given below.

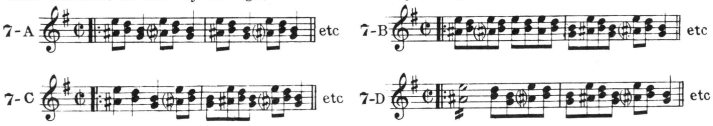

This entire lesson is to develop playing with FOUR-HAMMERS. Four hammers are generally used to feature SLOW MELODIES, BALLADS, etc. and some very beautiful effects may be had by playing these melodies, ballads, etc. with a sustained roll. With FOUR HAMMERS, a FOUR NOTE CHORD may be featured throughout. The illustrated folder contained in this lesson will give the positions of the hands, how to properly hold the hammers, how to SPREAD the hammers, etc. Read this folder carefully. Take your hammers, and adjust them to the different positions in these photographs. If necessary, put this folder in front of you when you are practicing. By doing this, you can compare your positions with the photographs. The most important thing in four-hammer playing is a good, smooth ROLL, and especially to be able to roll smoothly when the hammers are spread far apart. The roll with FOUR HAMMERS is the same principle as the ROLL with TWO HAMMERS. Many pupils think that the ROLL with FOUR HAMMERS is done by twisting the wrists, thereby striking the hammers at FOUR DIFFERENT INTERVALS. THIS IS WRONG. The CORRECT roll with FOUR HAMMERS is made as follows:-

THE ROLL AS WRITTEN:　　　　　THE ROLL AS PLAYED　　　etc.

The two lower notes are struck TOGETHER with the two hammers in the LEFT HAND, and the two upper notes are struck with the hammers in the RIGHT HAND. The SPEED of this roll should be the same as all other rolls.

The following exercises, No. 1, 2, 3, 4 and 5 are to be practiced until the ROLL becomes very smooth, and the different spreads worked out. You will find that the ROLL becomes more difficult when the hammers are spread far apart. Constant practice will overcome this. Repeat these exercises many times without stopping. Give FOUR counts or beats to each measure, and PLAY SLOWLY and SMOOTHLY. Always play the two UPPER notes with the RIGHT HAND, and the two LOWER notes with the LEFT HAND.

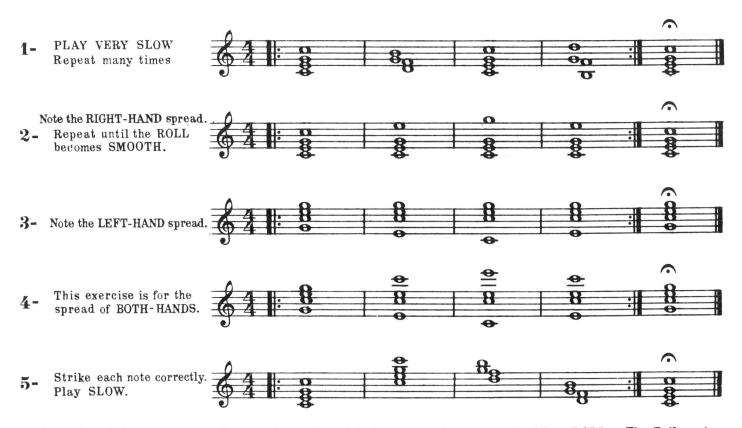

1- PLAY VERY SLOW
Repeat many times

2- Note the RIGHT-HAND spread.
Repeat until the ROLL becomes SMOOTH.

3- Note the LEFT-HAND spread.

4- This exercise is for the spread of BOTH-HANDS.

5- Strike each note correctly.
Play SLOW.

NOTE:- All whole notes and half notes throughout this lesson are to be played with a ROLL. The Roll marks have been omitted in this lesson in order to facilitate easier sight-reading.

Exercise 6 is to develop the SPREAD in each hand. This exercise is to be practiced first with ONE HAND and then with the OTHER HAND. Use only one hand at a time on this exercise. Repeat many times. Strike all notes correctly. Gradually increase the speed.

Exercises 7 and 8 are to be played with THREE HAMMERS. In exercise 7, use TWO HAMMERS in the RIGHT-HAND and ONE HAMMER in the left hand. This exercise is to develop the SPREAD in the RIGHT-HAND. The idea of this entire lesson is to develop a SMOOTH ROLL with FOUR HAMMERS. Therefore, DON'T PLAY FAST. Memorize this exercise, then look down at the Keyboard and play many times, each day.

In exercise 8, use TWO HAMMERS in the LEFT-HAND and ONE HAMMER in the RIGHT-HAND.

Exercise 9 is to develop the ROLL when playing chords where the notes are close together. The illustrated folder will show how the hammers are manipulated when playing two notes that are only ONE TONE apart. Repeat this exercise many times.

9- Practice with a
SLOW, EVEN ROLL.

Exercise 10 contains a melody that will give good practice as to playing with the hammers CLOSE TOGETHER. The two UPPER NOTES are to be taken with the RIGHT-HAND and the two LOWER NOTES are to be taken with the LEFT-HAND. Memorize this melody, then practice many times each day, FROM MEMORY. DON'T TRY TO PLAY FAST, use a ROLL in each measure throughout.

10

Exercise 11 contains a melody that will give good practice as to playing with the hammers SPREAD APART. Memorize, then practice from memory. Use a ROLL throughout, and play at a SLOW, EVEN TEMPO. Count FOUR to each measure.

11- Count four beats to
each measure, Play
slowly and smoothly.

FOUR HAMMER PLAYING. In order to play all chords in all Keys with FOUR - HAMMERS, it is necessary to turn the hands around, sometimes to a seemingly awkward position, in order to play the chords that are desired. This lesson gives material that will benefit these "TURNS" of the hands. The "TURN" is accomplished by turning the hands around, with the elbows well out, until the hammers are pointing in toward the body. You may find, at first, that it is very difficult to produce a smooth roll with the hands turned in this manner, but constant practice will enable you to overcome this difficulty. The illustrated folder pertaining to lessons 46 and 47 will give all the necessary information regarding the "TURN".

Exercises Nos. 1 and 2 contain a THREE NOTE CHORD and are to be practiced with THREE HAMMERS. Exercise No. 1 is to be practiced with TWO HAMMERS in the RIGHT - HAND and ONE HAMMER in the LEFT- HAND. Exercise No. 2 is to be practiced with ONE HAMMER in the RIGHT-HAND and TWO HAMMERS in the LEFT-HAND. Do not use the "TURN" in these two exercises. Keep the hands straight. Strike the sharps and flats on the ends of the bars. Employ a SMOOTH ROLL, SLOW TEMPO. Repeat many times.

Exercises Nos. 3-4-5 and 6 are to develop the "TURN". You will note that these four exercises are written in the Key of F MAJOR. When turning the hands, be sure and turn the hands well a- round, with the elbows out. Bend over the Key board, and you will be able to turn the hands further. So as to avoid confusion in these turns, note the following. In the 2nd measure of exercise No. 2., the two bottom notes, which are G and Bb, are struck with the left hand, as follows., The hammer held between the THUMB and FIRST FINGER striking the note G, and the hammer held between the 1st and 2nd fingers striking the note Bb. This is the proper position of the LEFT HAND when turned around. The RIGHT-HAND turn is done in the same manner. Repeat these exercises many times each day. Take plenty of time, and play SLOW. You cannot "RUSH" these turns and get results.

Note:- Roll on all notes in this lesson. The ROLL MARKS have been eliminated so as to facilitate easier sight reading.

Exercise No. 7 is in CHROMATIC FORM and the TURNS are all with the LEFT HAND. Practice at a very slow tempo, so as to get a smooth roll on each chord. The turns are marked on the chords where they are to be used. Memorize this exercise, then practice by looking down at the Key-board. This will enable you to watch your hands.

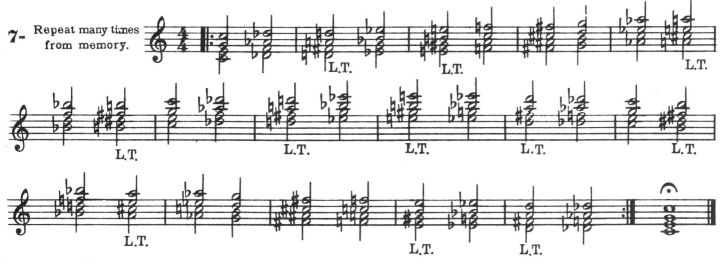

Examples 7-A and 7-B are starters on other four-note chords. Take any four-note chord that you wish, and play it in CHROMATIC FORM by modulating ONE HALF TONE at a time. TURN the hands whenever needed.

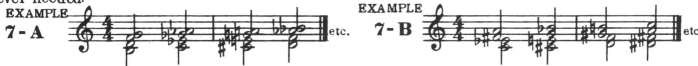

Exercise 8 contains a melody similar to the average waltz melody (CHORUS.) You will note that the OCTAVE CHORD is used throughout this melody. The octave chord means that the two outside notes in the chord are one octave apart, and the remaining two notes in the middle are to give what ever harmony is necessary to the melody. This is a good form to follow in playing melodies similar to this one. Learn this exercise by memory, then play many times each day, always at a SLOW TEMPO. Feature a smooth, even roll.

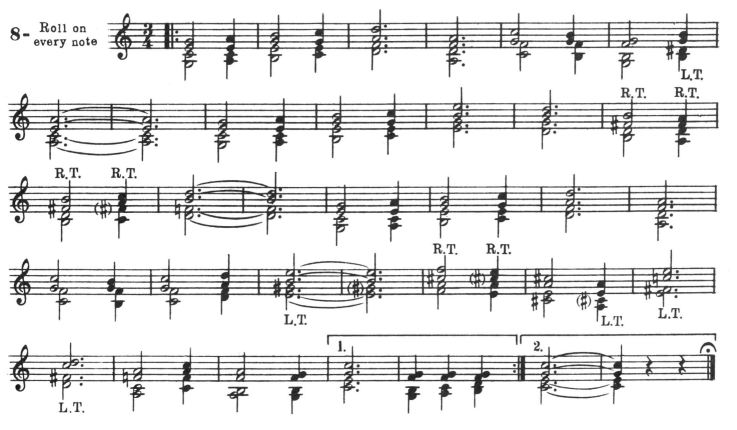

Exercise 9 is written in the Key of C major in $\frac{4}{4}$ time. In this exercise, a CLOSER chord is featured. In other words, the spread is less than one octave. There is no set rule to follow on this. You may use an octave chord, or you may spread more than an octave or less than an octave, assuming of course that the harmony is always correct. Learn this exercise by memory, then play several times each day. Note the TURNS. Employ a SMOOTH ROLL. - SLOW TEMPO.

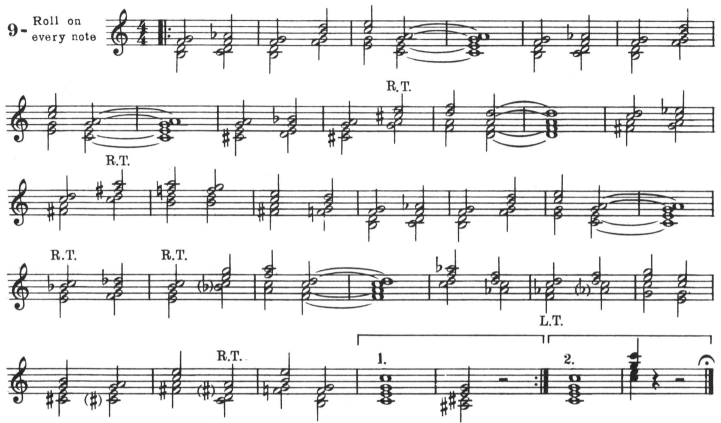

Note:- In the above exercise No. 9, strike the sharps and flats either on the ends of the bars or in the middle. On a slow, sustained ROLL, either way is correct.

Exercise No. 10 gives furthur practice as to the TURN with both hands. This exercise is only for practice, as otherwise it would not be practical to turn the hands on a C major chord, such as in the second measure. Roll on each chord in exercise No. 10. Note the turns which appear in every other measure. Turn both hands well around with the elbows OUT. The first measure is to be played with the hands STRAIGHT, in a natural position. Then in the 2nd measure, turn both hands, then the 3rd measure straight, fourth measure TURN, etc. throughout. Don't forget, a SLOW, SUSTAINED ROLL on each chord.

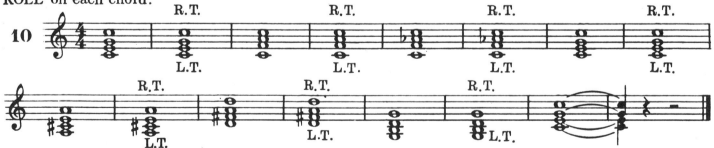

Exercise No. 11 is to be practiced WITHOUT a roll. Strike each chord once. Count a SLOW FOUR to each measure. Alternate the TURN as follows:- The 1st chord struck with the hands in a straight position, the 2nd chord with the hands TURNED, the 3rd chord STRAIGHT, the 4th chord TURNED and so on throughout. These exercises will give excellent practice on the "TURN."

This lesson will give ideas as to TRICK RHYTHMS. There is no limit as to how many trick rhythms there are. Anyone may invent any amount of them. The easiest plan to follow is this:- First work out the ideas in ¾ time (*Waltz time*), and then play the same notes in 4/4 time (*Fox-Trot time*). Here is an example:- Take TWO EIGHTH NOTES and TWO QUARTER NOTES and play them in waltz time, with the eighth notes coming first. Thus you have a measure in ¾ time. Then play this SAME MEASURE several times, as in FIGURE A. Now take these same notes as in FIGURE A, and by removing the lines between the notes, which designate the measures, and placing these lines EVERY FOUR QUARTER NOTES APART, you then have THE SAME NOTES in 4/4 time (*Fox-Trot time*), as in FIGURE B. This system will permit the invention of many TRICK RHYTHMS.

FIGURE A  FIGURE B

To simplify matters, we will refer to the notes in these TRICK RHYTHMS as FAST NOTES and SLOW NOTES. To make the rhythms different, change the fast notes, which in FIG.A, are the EIGHTH-NOTES, and play TRIPLETS instead. (*See Exercise No.1.*) Then, to get more variety, instead of starting with the FAST NOTES, start with the SLOW NOTES (*Quarter Notes.*) This is done in EXERCISES NO.2 and 3. Memorize these exercises and then compare them. In this way you will get the idea of these trick rhythms.

1. Practice many times each day. Strike all notes correctly. Observe the QUARTER NOTES as to their proper count.

2. Notice that the FAST NOTES come on the SECOND QUARTER BEAT in the first measure. Practice many times.

3 Notice that the FAST NOTES come on the THIRD QUARTER BEAT in the first measure. Practice many times.

148

In Exercise No.4 the first and second quarter beats in the first measure contain FAST NOTES, and the third quarter beat contains a SLOW NOTE. You will also note that in this example the fast notes are composed of both TRIPLETS and DOTTED EIGHTH-NOTES. This exercise can be played in a different rhythm by simply changing the time-value of the notes. For EXAMPLE:- instead of starting with the TRIPLET, start with the DOTTED EIGHTH-NOTES, then the TRIPLET second, and then the QUARTER NOTE. But DON'T CHANGE THE NOTES, only change the

time-value of them. LIKE THIS:-

First learn these melodies as they are written before you try to change the rhythm.

4. Practice many times each day. Memorize. Note the Key of F, (One Flat)

The idea in changing these rhythms is that you DON'T change the MELODY, you only change the rhythm. After you thoroughly learn these different melodies, then take some manuscript paper and invent some different rhythms to these same notes in these melodies. The instructions given to Ex. No.4 will show how you can do this.

5. Note the Key of B FLAT (Two Flats). Observe the quarter notes as to their proper count.

In Ex. No.5, a group of FOUR DOTTED EIGHTH NOTES are given throughout, and in Ex. No.6, TWO GROUPS OF TRIPLETS are given. You will notice that these examples are given in different Keys. This is done to give you the benefit of playing in different Keys. All of these examples should be practiced several days, even though they may seem easy.

6. Note the Key of E FLAT (Three Flats) Memorize

TRICK RHYTHMS may also be applied in the form of DOUBLE-NOTE ragtime. Examples 7-A and 7-B will give the two most commonly used forms. Practice these two examples until the rhythms can be played perfectly smooth, and at a modern FOX-TROT TEMPO.   If necessary, count FOUR to each measure, then when the rhythms become familiar, count TWO to each measure.

7-A Note the Key of G (*One Sharp*) Repeat many times.

7-B Repeat many times.

7. Practice many times Strike every note correctly, memorize.

Don't forget:- after you have thoroughly learned these different melodies in this lesson, take some music paper, and write out the SAME NOTES in different rhythms. Substitute TRIPLETS in place of the STRAIGHT EIGHTH-NOTES, and so on. If you do this, you will greatly benefit your ability to play modern ragtime rhythms.   Write out your inventions in DIFFERENT KEYS.

8. Repeat many times, memorize, then play from memory.

ALWAYS TAKE THE FIRST ENDING TO REPEAT.

In this lesson a melody, similar to the average fox-trot melody, such as played for dancing, is given. In many dance melodies, the construction is such that a "BREAK" can be featured in the middle of the melody (*chorus*). This idea of the "break" is also given in this lesson. Exercise No.1 contains the straight melody, such as is contained in the average dance melody. Practice and learn to play this melody just as it is, FROM MEMORY. This is important. You must memorize and perfect this straight melody, so that you will be able to compare it with the ragtime versions and variations to it. Practice it in strict tempo, and always take the 1st ending to repeat. Work it up to about a fox-trot, dance tempo. Strike all notes correctly, and observe the dotted-eighth notes. DON'T play TOO FAST.

Examples 1A - 2A - 3A - 4A - 5A - 6A - 7A - 8A - 9A and 10-A will give ten different "BREAKS" to feature in the 7th and 8th measures of Exercise No.1. These breaks should all be memorized. When you play Ex. No.1, play it as written until you come to the 7th and 8th measures, then put in one of these "BREAKS" and then continue on throughout to the end of the melody. It is understood, of course, that the BREAK must be played in the SAME TEMPO as the entire exercise. Don't slow down when you come to the break. Play it the same as if it were written in the exercise. (*7th and 8th bars*) Any one of these breaks will fit the melody. Use any one you wish. When repeating, use different breaks each time you repeat.

Exercise No.2 contains a ragtime version of the melody contained in Exercise No.1. This ragtime version is written in STRAIGHT EIGHTH-NOTES. I am assuming that you now know the melody in Exercise No.1. by memory. In comparing the two exercises you will notice that Exercise No.2 contains practically the same melody as in Ex.No.1. with the exception that it is played in ragtime. It by comparison that you will acquire the best ideas on improving, therefore, memorize this exercise. The "BREAK" is also featured in this exercise. In selecting a BREAK for this exercise, select the ones that are similar in rhythm. BREAKS 1-A, 2-A, 3-A and 4-A are best suited to this exercise.

You will notice that in exercise No.2, a RIGHT-HAND RHYTHM is featured throughout. Exercise No.3 gives another ragtime version of this same melody contained in Exercise No.1 This exercise features a ragtime rhythm with both hands doing about the same amount of work. Any rhythm can be applied to a melody similar to these examples. The two important points to consider are these, namely:– The rhythm must be in tempo and it harmonize with the melody.

Exercise No.4. contains a "SLAP" version of the melody in Exercise No.1. You will notice by comparing these different rhythms with the melody in Exercise No.1 that they all HARMONIZE with the melody. As long as you harmonize with the melody, you can feature ANY RHYTHM that you wish. Note the accents in this exercise. Repeat many times.

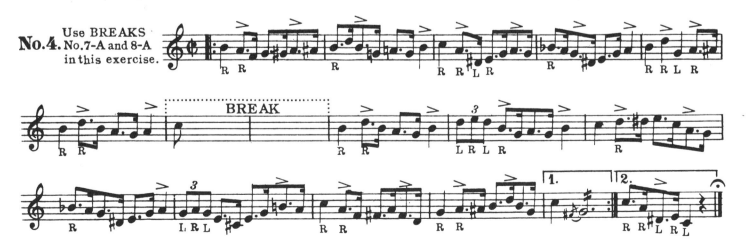

Exercise No. 5 is a VARIATION to the melody in Exercise No. 1. In this variation, DOTTED EIGHTH-NOTES are featured throughout. The same rule prevails as to variations. Harmonize with the melody and you may use any form of rhythm or variation that you wish. Practice each one of these exercises thoroughly until it can be played from memory. DON'T rush the tempo.

No. 5. Use BREAKS 7-A and 8-A in this exercise.

Exercise No. 6 contains a variation to the melody in Exercise No. 1. In this variation, TRIPLETS and DOTTED EIGHTH-NOTES are used. This is one of the best forms of variation to apply to a fox-trot melody. Practice along this idea:— Play the straight melody in Ex. No. 1, then repeat and play one of these variation Exercises, then repeat again and play a ragtime version, etc.

No. 6. Use BREAK 9-A in this exercise

Exercise No. 7 contains a variation form in which SIXTEENTH-NOTES are featured. In order to apply this exercise, play at a SLOWER TEMPO. Every note must be struck correcty, therefore, play slow at first. Alternate by playing Exercise No. 1, then this variation, then No. 1 again, then another variation. A good plan to follow is to start at the beginning of this lesson and every time you repeat, take a different version of the melody. Use any BREAKS that you wish.

No. 7.

In this lesson, final advice and examples pertaining to IMPROVISING are given. By following the advice and examples, you will be able to improvise and build up any melody to suit your own ideas. Read over carefully all instructions and advice contained in this lesson before practicing. Example 1 contains a melody with a verse and chorus, similar to the average FOX-TROT melody that is played for dancing. This example is similar to the TOP-LINE (TREBLE CLEF) of the average Piano part from the orchestration. The piano-part has been selected because it gives the CORRECT HARMONY together with the melody. By comparing this example with the TOP-LINE (TREBLE CLEF) of any piano part taken from a dance orchestration, you will see that the construction of the two parts are practically the same. Many pupils complain that the average piano-part appears confusing, owing to so many notes, etc. However, this lesson will give to you a system whereby you will be able to take any melody that you wish and work it out step by step until you can play it in whatever style may appeal to you. Take the examples in this lesson in the order in which they come, and compare each one with the original melody contained on this page (EXAMPLE - 1.)

In order to properly IMPROVISE a melody, and apply to it whatever ragtime rhythms, variations, etc. that may appeal to you, it is necessary that FIRST you learn the correct melody, as it is written, and also the CORRECT HARMONY that goes with the melody. Example 2 contains the melody and harmony note taken from Example-1. The easiest system to follow in order to harmonize a melody is this:- The TOP-NOTE throughout Example 1 is the melody. In selecting the harmony note to go with it, select the harmony note that is NEAREST the melody note. Then, when you play the two notes together, play them in the rhythm of the MELODY-NOTE. Here is an example:- Compare the first measures of Examples 1 and 2. You will notice that the top note (MELODY-NOTE) is the same. In Example 1 there are TWO HARMONY NOTES to select from, and you will notice in Example 2 that the harmony note NEAREST the melody note is used. Now compare the second measures of Examples 1 and 2. The melody note is the same, of course, and the nearest note to the melody is used (B FLAT.) The melody note in this measure is a WHOLE NOTE, therefore make the harmony note also a whole note. In this way the harmony-note is played in the same rhythm as the melody note. IMPORTANT. It is not necessary that you always select the harmony note NEAREST to the melody. Any note contained in the piano-part will harmonize, but it is best form to keep the two notes close together as much as possible.

NOTE:- In the thirteenth measure of the CHORUS, the harmony note F SHARP is used. Although this is not the nearest harmony note to the melody, it is the PREDOMINATING note of the chord, and for this reason, it is used. (Compare the thirteenth measures of Examples 1 and 2.)

Before starting to practice Example 3 it is necessary that you are able to play perfectly, Example - 2. Thus you have something to work on. The first step to take in order to apply ragtime to this melody is as follows. The measures which contain WHOLE-NOTES, HALF-NOTES or both, play them in a RAGTIME RHYTHM instead of sustaining them with the ROLL. Use any ragtime rhythm that you have had throughout the entire course. The rhythm used here is one of the most used forms of double note ragtime. The measures which contain the QUARTER-NOTES, EIGHTH-NOTES, in other words, the motion of the melody, PLAY THESE MEASURES AS WRITTEN. DON'T apply ragtime to the measures containing the FAST-NOTES. Only apply ragtime to the measures containing the SLOW-NOTES. This is the first step to work out. It is understood, of course, that the harmony MUST AT NO PLACE be changed. By working out this example, you are simply ADDING TO WHAT YOU ALREADY HAVE IN EXAMPLE - 2. Compare this example - 3 with example - 2. Then you will see that every measure containing the SUSTAINED part of the melody is played in RAGTIME RHYTHM instead of a ROLL. All the other measures containing the MOTION of the melody, are exactly the same as in Example - 2.

Practice and learn this example until it can be played from memory, in strict FOX-TROT TEMPO. Then compare with Example - 2 in order to see which measures have the RAGTIME RHYTHM applied to them.

Example 3 gives a system that can be applied to any fox-trot melody, and in any key namely, by playing the sustained parts of the melody in ragtime instead of a ROLL. Example-4 shows how the ENTIRE MELODY is played in ragtime. Both the sustained and the motion parts of the melody are played in ragtime form. There is no rule as to which ragtime rhythm must be used; USE ANY RHYTHM THAT YOU WISH, SO LONG AS IT HARMONIZES WITH THE MELODY AND IS IN ACCORDANCE WITH THE TEMPO. You will note that in this example, the melody of Example 1 is plainly in evidence. In other words, the melody is plainly distinguished throughout. This is an important factor to always consider. STICK TO THE MELODY. Play all the ragtime you wish, but play it on the MELODY and HARMONY NOTES. It is just as easy to apply ragtime to these two notes as to any others, and by adhering to this rule, you not only feature ragtime, but you feature the melody as well. Study and practice this example until it can be played in dance tempo, from memory. Then compare it with Examples 1-2 and 3.

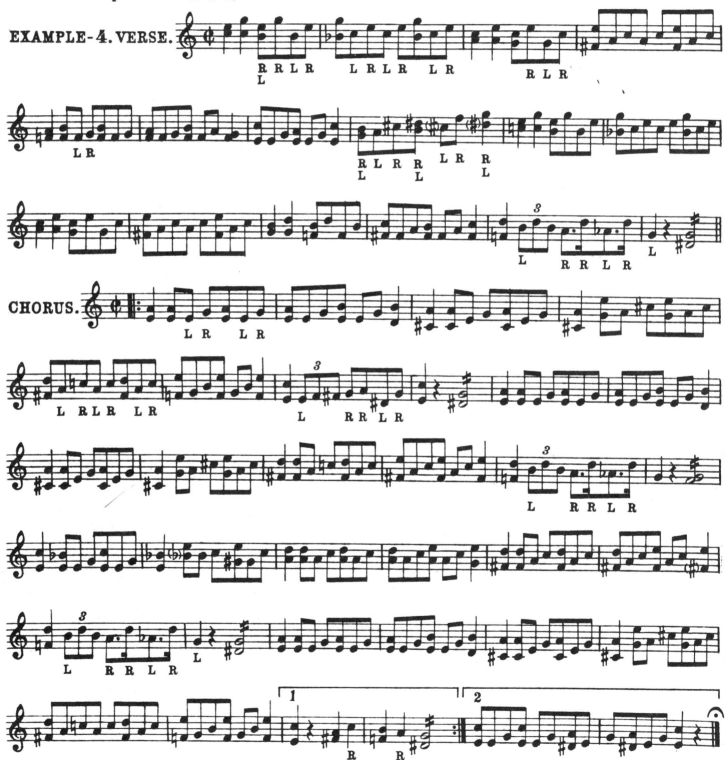

Example - **5** contains a ragtime version of this same melody in Example **1**, wherein TRIP-LETS and occasionally DOTTED EIGHTH NOTES are used. As usual, the MELODY is plainly in evidence. Practice and study this example until it can be played from memory and in dance tempo. Then, turn to EXAMPLE **1**, read from that page and play THIS EXAMPLE. DO THIS WITH ALL THE EXAMPLES IN THIS LESSON. Practicing along these ideas will prove a big help to IMPROVISING. These different examples MUST be worked out step by step in order that you fully understand these ideas. Many different ideas may be worked out from these examples by simply making a slight change. In FIGURE A, the TRIPLET is taken out and a quarter rest substituted. Play the entire EXAMPLE - **5** this way. Wherever the TRIPLET appears, DON'T PLAY IT. Count a quarter-rest instead. FIGURE B is just the reverse of FIGURE A. In FIGURE B, play the TRIPLET and take out the last three eighth-notes in the measure.

NOTE:- Learn to play EXAMPLE **5** from memory before experimenting with FIGURES A and B.

In EXAMPLE - **6**, a simple form of variation is used. This example contains the CHORUS of EXAMPLE - **1**. In this example, the VARIATION FORM is applied only to the measures which contain the sustained parts of the melody, such as whole-notes. The other measures are the same as the original melody. This system can be applied to any melody and in any key. Any form of variation may be used, so long as it HARMONIZES with the melody. In EXAMPLE **6**, triplets and dotted eighth-notes are used. Learn to play this example from memory, then read from EXAMPLE **1** and play this variation.

EXAMPLE-6. CHORUS.

Example - **7** contains a variation to ALL measures in the chorus, both the sustained measures and the measures containing the motion of the melody. Memorize this example, and then read from EXAMPLE **1** and play this variation. Don't try to play these variations TOO FAST.

EXAMPLE-7. CHORUS.

Example 8 contains a variation to the chorus wherein TRIPLETS are featured throughout. Triplets in variation form are the best to apply to the average dance melody. Study and practice this example until it can be played from memory, then read from EXAMPLE - 1 and play this example - 8. when playing variations, always bear in mind this fact, namely:- Use any form that you wish, either TRIPLETS, SIXTEENTH NOTES, DOTTED EIGHTH NOTES,etc. but always HARMONIZE with the melody. It is not necessary that you feature the melody, but at all times your variation must harmonize with the melody.

Example - 9 gives an idea as to how an accompaniment may be played. This idea is used when some other instrument in the orchestra is featuring the melody. In this idea the xylo-phone DOES NOT feature the melody. You simply FILL IN with whatever notes other than the melody will harmonize, and bring out an AFTER-BEAT EFFECT.

Memorize all of these examples, and then compare them with the original melody in Example - 1. Don't forget to always play the 1st endings to repeat.

Final Instructions

In this final lesson, my aim is to give ideas that will enable you to improvise any melody that you care to. Therefore, my advice is that you spend several weeks, if necessary, on this lesson until you have mastered each example and can play them all from memory. Then take any popular melody and work it out similar to the routine given in this lesson. Write out your different ideas step by step, the same as I have done in this lesson. In this way you may continue to study indefinitely.

Select any popular melody that appeals to you, and in any key. I suggest the piano-accompaniment part from the dance orchestration as the best part to work from. Take a sheet of manuscript paper (music paper) and copy the melody from the printed part, JUST AS IT IS WRITTEN. Then select a harmony note that is near to the melody note and write it in your manuscript beneath the melody note. Where the printed part contains three or four harmony notes, select the one that most clearly brings out the harmony. Complete your entire melody according to this routine, and then learn to play it from memory. This will give you the complete melody in double-notes, and this should be done FIRST with every melody that you work on.

Now take another sheet of manuscript paper, and go over your melody again, and wherever the melody contains a SUS-TAINED PART, apply a ragtime rhythm to it. You may apply any rhythm that appeals to you. The remainder of the melody, which completes the MOTION, is to be played exactly as in your first copy. Complete the entire melody this way and you then have the melody with the unsustained parts in ragtime and the other parts as written. Then practice and learn to play from memory what you have written out.

Now take another sheet of manuscript paper, go over the melody again, and apply ragtime rhythms to EVERY MEASURE. You already have the sustained measures in ragtime, therefore, copy these measures just as they are and work out all the other measures in a similar way. It is not necessary that you exactly follow the rhythm of the melody when applying ragtime rhythms to it. Occasionally it is necessary to change the rhythm of the melody in order to work out a good idea as to ragtime. (The 2nd and 4th measures in the chorus of Example 4 will show what is meant here.) After you have completed your melody in this manner, practice and learn to play it from memory.

The next step is to elaborate on what you have worked out. Example 5, with the instructions contained therein, will explain how this is done. After you work out your melodies in ragtime rhythms, and have them all written down, then go ahead and change the rhythms. Add more notes to them and feature TRIPLETS, etc. Take any of the rhythms that you have had in any of the former lessons and apply them to the melody and harmony as notes that you have worked out. If you will work out these ideas one at a time and WRITE OUT your steps as you go along, you will soon note a big improvement in your ability to improvise. Remember, practice makes perfect, and where the first few melodies may seem difficult, they will become easier as you progress.

Variations are applied to a melody in the same manner as ragtime rhythms. Work out your variations in a very easy form first, such as quarter-notes. Any form of arpeggio, scale or broken-chord will do, so long as it harmonizes with your melody. WRITE THEM OUT, then you can check up on what you have written and make changes for the better. In this way, with the proper amount of study, you will gradually build up your ideas until they are just what you want. Don't be discouraged if these variations, rhythms, etc. seem difficult at first. If you will start at the bottom and work up, step by step, you will gradually get to a point where the entire idea of improvising will seem easy.

As this routine entails considerable writing, your work will be easier if you use good materials. I suggest ten or twelve line manuscript paper, and preferably ten line paper for easier writing. I use a Spencerian-Congressional Pen Point, No. 28, for all writing of music. A good music ink for all work is Moore's Music Ink. Any pen-holder will do.